Synthesis Lectures on Data Management

Series Editor

H. V. Jagadish, University of Michigan, Ann Arbor, MI, USA

This series publishes lectures on data management. Topics include query languages, database system architectures, transaction management, data warehousing, XML and databases, data stream systems, wide scale data distribution, multimedia data management, data mining, and related subjects.

Pingcheng Ruan · Tien Tuan Anh Dinh ·
Dumitrel Loghin · Meihui Zhang · Gang Chen

Blockchains

Decentralized and Verifiable Data Systems

 Springer

Pingcheng Ruan
Department of Computer Science
National University of Singapore
Singapore, Singapore

Tien Tuan Anh Dinh
Singapore University of Technology
and Design
Singapore, Singapore

Dumitrel Loghin
Department of Computer Science
National University of Singapore
Singapore, Singapore

Meihui Zhang
Beijing Institute of Technology
Beijing, China

Gang Chen
Zhejiang University
Hangzhou, China

ISSN 2153-5418 ISSN 2153-5426 (electronic)
Synthesis Lectures on Data Management
ISBN 978-3-031-13981-9 ISBN 978-3-031-13979-6 (eBook)
https://doi.org/10.1007/978-3-031-13979-6

This Springer imprint is published by the registered company Springer Nature Switzerland AG
The registered company address is: Gewerbestrasse 11, 6330 Cham, Switzerland

Foreword

Blockchain technology and systems have been at the center of computer science in the last decade, receiving enormous attention and perhaps even a greater amount of controversy. The main cause for the latter is due to the use of blockchain in cryptocurrencies, which has been touted to disrupt the existing financial systems. At the same time, the technology is itself a game changer, as it opens up the space for practical data systems that support immutability and verifiability.

As data systems, blockchains face unique challenges introduced by the presence of untrusted servers. The decentralized architectures call for the rethinking and redesigning of many components in traditional databases. The focus on security makes blockchains robust against attacks, which renders them attractive for many applications that require a high degree of trustworthiness from the underlying data platform. For data engineers, blockchains are secure transactional platforms. For entrepreneurs, blockchains bring opportunities for starting the next unicorn companies, as well as for improving existing systems.

This book is timely as it serves as a tutorial on blockchain systems, with a focus on the similarities and differences between blockchains and distributed database systems. It serves as a reference to researchers and engineers who want to push the fusion of the technologies further. I hope you will enjoy reading the book as much as I did.

Beng Chin Ooi

Preface

Blockchains have taken the world by storm. Everything started with a mysterious user with the pseudo-name Satoshi Nakamoto, who proposed an electronic payment system called Bitcoin. The system is peer-to-peer and single-handedly brings cryptocurrency into the mainstream. Bitcoin's underpinning technology, the blockchain, has also brought renewed interest in decentralized systems. A decentralized system has no single owner, and all the stakeholders contribute to the system's robustness. Blockchains can be used to build trust into existing systems, thus they present attractive solutions in many different domains, spanning both academia and industry. Despite this potential, we have not seen high-impact, real-world applications of blockchain other than cryptocurrencies. What are the fundamental, technical limitations that are preventing blockchain from realizing its full potential?

In this book, we set out to demystify blockchains through the lens of database systems. This perspective carries two benefits. First, databases are extensively researched and field tested for many years; therefore, using database concepts to explain blockchain systems allows for a deeper understanding of the latter. Secondly, using the connection between databases and blockchains from the start helps emphasize the focus of the book, which is on blockchain as a general platform rather than one that is specifically designed for cryptocurrency. We believe that blockchain, as a novel data system, has the potential to disrupt main industry sectors, just as databases did decades ago.

Who Should Read This Book?

We assume our readers are familiar with basic computer science and database concepts, including transactions with ACID properties, Merkle trees, and asymmetric encryption. To cater to those without sufficient security background, we have compiled all relevant basic cryptographic primitives in Appendix A.1. In particular, the book targets students, researchers, and engineers with a computer science background. Readers who are completely new to blockchains will find this book useful as it contains a comprehensive survey of the state of the art. Readers who have some experience with blockchains, for example from using or developing cryptocurrencies, may find the book's database perspectives enlightening. Finally, researchers working in the blockchain space will be able to appreciate the design space and the subtle differences with state-of-the-art databases. They can identify gaps in the space and explore potential solutions that create next-generation blockchain systems.

What Content Is There in This Book?

A blockchain is essentially a novel data processing system that consists of multiple servers (or nodes), and some of the servers do not behave as expected. Our book compares and contrasts blockchains against distributed database systems.

First, the presence of Byzantine nodes makes it challenging to ensure the robustness of a distributed database. Our book discusses these challenges, which include how to provide Byzantine-tolerant consensus during replication, how to avoid anomalies under concurrency, how to ensure storage integrity, and how to perform secure sharding. Second, blockchains contain unique features that are not found in traditional database systems. We discuss these new features, such as payment channels (Sect. 3.5.1), that are possible because of the incentives mechanism and security guarantees of blockchains.

Our book focuses on the systems and data management aspects of blockchains. We distill the insights from referenced works published in top systems venues, such as SIGMOD, VLDB, SOSP, NSDI, KDD, and OSDI. We do not focus on the networking layer of the blockchains, as discussed in [92, 139]. When describing systems that use advanced cryptographic primitives, such as ZK-SNARK, we assume the primitives are secure and only focus on how the system exploits their properties for security.

How Is the Book Organized?

Blockchains follow the development phases that are observed in every ground-breaking technology. Once a breakthrough leaps into the spotlight, scientists and researchers devote themselves to unfolding its fundamentals, deepening its understanding, formulating theories, and creating more knowledge. At the same time, engineers work on implementing it for wider and practical purposes. The technological advancements are underpinned by research-discovered knowledge, which then bring improvements to existing applications and give rise to new ones. As our pedagogical methodology, we rely on this lifecycle to streamline the whole book. We have summarized the book chapters with respect to blockchain's phases in Fig. 1.

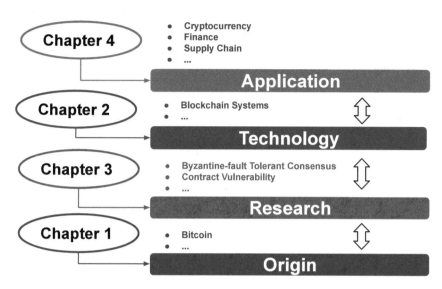

Fig. 1 The origin and evolution of blockchains, and the corresponding chapters in this book

1. Chapter 1 reviews the blockchains' origin and evolution. It follows the history of blockchain, which starts from a decentralized payment system, namely Bitcoin, then evolves to general decentralized computing platforms, e.g., Ethereum, and reaches the current state of systems optimized for both security and performance.

2. Chapter 2 focuses on the technical aspects of blockchains. We discuss them within a framework that unifies blockchains and distributed database systems. In this framework, blockchains and distributed databases are transactional data processing systems with different design trade-offs. Specifically, blockchains prioritize security, while distributed databases prioritize performance. As transactional systems, they address similar sets of challenges, but we discuss how they differ in their approaches due to the design trade-offs. Our discussion focuses on four main design components: replication, concurrency, storage, and sharding.

3. Chapter 3 expands on the research frontier of blockchains by discussing the state-of-the-art techniques for the four design components introduced in Chap. 2. We focus on techniques that strengthen the system's robustness and improve the overall performance.

4. Chapter 4 discusses applications built on top of blockchains. We select four representative domains, namely finance, healthcare, supply chain, and identity management. We identify the current pain points that blockchains help alleviate. The section also contains an analysis of the obstacles that blockchains need to overcome to fully realize their potentials.

We sincerely hope that this book inspires a new generation of blockchain researchers who push the boundary and bring about the next technological breakthrough.

Singapore, Singapore   Pingcheng Ruan
Singapore, Singapore   Tien Tuan Anh Dinh
Singapore, Singapore   Dumitrel Loghin
Beijing, China   Meihui Zhang
Hangzhou, China   Gang Chen

Contents

List of Figures

List of Tables

Origin and Evolution

The origin of blockchains can be traced back to Bitcoin [220]. We start this chapter with a review of Bitcoin. We first explain its core data structure which is a ledger comprising of multiple blocks. We then expand on its core innovation, namely the Proof-of-Work (PoW) consensus protocol, which allows mutually distrusting peers to securely agree on a common history. Starting from Bitcoin, blockchains branched out in two directions: one that retains the security of Bitcoin but extends its application beyond simple payment, for example, Ethereum [282], and the other that improves Bitcoin's performance with stronger trust assumptions, for example, Hyperledger Fabric [37], Quorum [53], and R3 Corda [54]. This chapter provides a high-level overview of these post-Bitcoin systems.

1.1 Let There Be Bitcoin

1.1.1 Ledger, Blocks, and Transactions

Figure 1.1 presents a high-level visualization of Bitcoin data structure. A ledger consists of a list of blocks, where each block is chained to the predecessor with a hash pointer. The `genesis block` refers to the first block in the ledger. Each block batches transactions as its payload. A block also includes other meta-fields, such as the block height in the ledger, in its header. Transactions encode the payment transfer. Hence, a ledger encapsulates a complete history of transactions. Its unique hash chain structure preserves the history integrity. Moreover, the consensus (detailed below) fully replicates such ledger in each peer. Besides Bitcoin, nearly all blockchain systems follow this decentralized chain structure. Hence, blockchains are often called `Decentralized Ledgers`.

We now turn back to Bitcoin and describe a transaction's structure. Conceptually, Bitcoin transactions embody monetary transfers. Transfers are technically backed up by cryptographic asymmetric encryption. The user's ownership of cryptocurrencies is represented

P. Ruan et al., *Blockchains*, Synthesis Lectures on Data Management,
https://doi.org/10.1007/978-3-031-13979-6_1

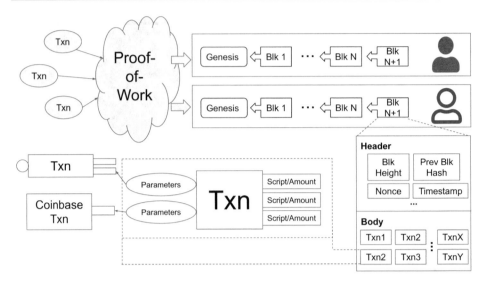

Fig. 1.1 A high-level visualization of the bitcoin ledger, blocks, and transactions. Transactions are proposed to a peer-to-peer network and then sequenced into a ledger. PoW replicates the ledger, in the form of hash-chained blocks, on each peer. A block consists of two parts, namely a header and a body. The former consists of various meta-fields, and the latter batches transactions. A transaction in Bitcoin consists of inputs and outputs. An output associates a cryptocurrency amount with validation scripts. An input references a previous transaction output. It also provides parameters to pass the output script checking. The illustrated transaction redeems the newly minted coins, as it references a coinbase transaction with no inputs

by the possession of a private key. The user address takes the form of the corresponding public key hash. Ownership can be proved with the corresponding digital signatures. Proof-of-ownership is a precondition for a sender to make the transfer.

In more technical details, a Bitcoin transaction consists of multiple inputs and outputs. An output is associated with a cryptocurrency amount and a script snippet. The script contains an address and encodes the qualifying conditions for future spenders. Correspondingly, an input references an output of a previous transaction. It also provides ownership evidence, such as a digital signature, to pass the script-encoded condition. Then, the input can redeem the output-associated cryptocurrencies. A valid transaction must ensure that the total input amount must exceed the total output amount. (As we shall see later, the surplus is regarded as the transaction fee, to be awarded to block proposers.) Factually, a transaction aggregates the cryptocurrencies from previous transactions, as referenced by its inputs. Then, it transfers them to addresses specified in its outputs. With this structure, a system state comprises a collection of Unspent Transaction Outputs (UTXO). Given this, we refer to this blockchain data model as UTXO.

Though output scripts can be in multiple forms, below we explain the most common `pay-to-public-key-hash` transaction. We describe how an input and an output interact to prove ownership. The output script looks like OP_DUP OP_HASH160 <Address> OP_EQUAL OP_CHECKSIG. To unlock its protected cryptocurrencies, the script expects two input-provided parameters, a digital signature, and a public key. The first two opcodes, OP_DUP OP_HASH160, instruct to duplicate the public key and compute the key hash. Then <Address> OP_EQUAL verifies whether the computed hash is consistent with the output-specified <Address>. In the end, the last opcode, OP_CHECKSIG, verifies the signature for the public key. In a nutshell, a qualified input provides a valid asymmetric key pair with the public key hash matching the output address.

1.1.2   Proof-of-Work and Mining

The previous section describes the structure of the ledger, blocks, and transactions. It specifies what legitimate blocks are like, in order to be eligible for the later-mentioned consensus. The involved hashed chain and asymmetric encryption are mature cryptographic techniques. These techniques can be dated back decades earlier than Bitcoin. What really makes Bitcoin stand out is Proof-of-Work (PoW), a simple yet effective consensus protocol. PoW drives mutually distrusting parties to synchronize toward a consistent chain made of blocks and transactions conform to the above specifications. In addition, the mutually distrusted assumption implies that some peers may not honestly follow the protocol. These peers are referred to as Byzantines. Despite this, PoW-equipped systems can still mask Byzantines and function as intended. In this section, we first lay out the consensus procedure. We then justify its effectiveness via a Q&A format.

In a nutshell, PoW requires peers to continuously compete in solving a puzzle. Concretely, the competition is a nonce-finding process for a block at the ledger tip. The nonce is a part of the block field. The target nonce must make the block hash prefixed with a certain number of zeros. We refer to the required number of zeroes as the difficulty level. The solution-finding process is referred to as *mining*. The first successful solver has the privilege to broadcast the tip block and it gets correspondingly compensated. Other peers first validate the legitimacy of the received block. Then, they apply it to extend their individually maintained ledger. Afterward, they continue mining on it, i.e., competing for the chain extension privilege. Nonetheless, it may happen that two or more peers propose different next blocks. This situation is called a blockchain *fork*. The fork with the longest chain is considered as the canonical ledger. In a word, non-Byzantine peers shall deem transactions in the longest chain as committed. We summarize the Proof-of-Work consensus in Fig. 1.2.

The above description lays out the intended behavior which an non-Byzantine peer shall follow, i.e., how to extend the ledger and treat transactions as committed. We now justify why this simple mechanism achieves a Byzantine consensus. In particular, why a rational peer may find it better to follow the protocol. And likewise, why malicious peers can never coalesce to derail the process. Throughout the below Q&A session, we always assume that non-Byzantine peers constitute the majority, where the majority is defined with respect to

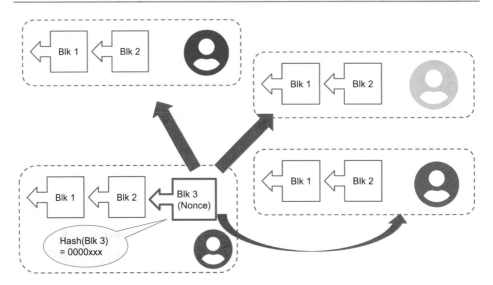

Fig. 1.2 Overview of proof-of-work consensus. Peers compete on mining at the ledger tip. Mining entails finding a binary (nonce) so that the block hash is prefixed with enough zeros. The first solver broadcasts the block to others in a P2P network. Others verify the received block and use it to extend their own chain, after which they proceed to mine for the next block. All the above actions are aligned for the best interest of their takers

the mining power. Additionally, it takes a maximum of δ time to broadcast a block to all the peers.

Why do rational peers tend to propose valid blocks, and why Byzantines cannot flood the system with invalid ones? A valid nonce is a precondition for a proposed block. It requires the block hash to be prefixed with enough zeros. Hash functions are preimage-resistant (that is, it is infeasible to find the input, or preimage, for a given hash output). Byzantines have no efficient ways other than guessing and testing for random nonces. Besides, hash computation is expensive. This prevents Byzantines from flooding the system with invalid blocks, as it is costly to them. From the perspective of rational peers, they have used many resources to find a nonce. They are economically inclined to ensure the block's validity so that they can get compensated for the expenditures.

How are non-Byzantine peers compensated? The compensation takes two forms, the coinbase transaction and transaction fee. The coinbase transaction is a special transaction that mints cryptocurrencies. Particularly, the protocol allows each block to include a unique transaction with no inputs and one output. The output can specify any address but its associated cryptocurrency amount is protocol-mandated. Block proposers can specify their address to claim the minted cryptocurrencies as their mining reward. Later, block proposers may reference the transaction output for their spending. The newly minted cryptocurrency amount is periodically halved so that the total sum converges.

The transaction fee is the sum of input-output amount differential of all transactions in a block. (Let us take the example of a block containing two transactions, $TxnA$ and $TxnB$. The total input amounts in $TxnA$ and $TxnB$ are $Input_A$ and $Input_B$, respectively. Their output amounts are $Output_A$ and $Output_B$, respectively. Then, the transaction fee in this block is computed as $(Output_A - Input_A) + (Output_B - Input_B)$.) The protocol also allows block proposers to create a likewise transaction that credits the transaction fee to their address. From the standpoint of the clients, transaction senders can increase the differential between their inputs and outputs. This is to economically attract block proposers to include their transactions.

Why does the longest fork remain stable despite Byzantines' manipulation, and why are non-Byzantine peers inclined to mine on the longest fork?

The Bitcoin protocol periodically adjusts the mining difficulty such that the block generation interval is far greater than δ. This ensures the synchronization of all the peers. In other words, all peers hold a consistent ledger view for most of the time. Assume the majority of the mining power is concentrated on the common longest fork. This fork will grow at a faster pace than any other fork. It is because the same difficulty level applies to all forks. As a consequence, it takes more time to produce a block in a chain fork with less power, despite the Byzantines' coalition. Rational clients can be reassured that the longest chain remains stable and its transactions can be safely considered committed. Likewise, non-Byzantine peers are incentivized to extend the chain. This is to get their compensations (coinbase transactions and fees) recognized.

How is the difficulty level adjusted? The number of required prefixed zeros controls the mining difficulty. The exact number is 10 for the genesis block and, at the time of writing this book, it is 19. The Bitcoin protocol adjusts this parameter at every 2016 blocks, pegging the expected block interval to 10 min. It is assumed that 10 min are enough for a block to be fully broadcasted in the network.

How does a chain fork occur? Why is it dangerous? How does it resolve? A chain fork, as exemplified in Fig. 1.3, occurs either from the Byzantines' attack to tumble the longest chain, or it is due to the rare occasion when two peers find the solution to the PoW challenge at almost the same time. It may also happen that a proposer mines a block before it is aware of another proposed block at the same height, e.g., due to a temporal network partition or an extremely small block interval. Unintentional chain bifurcation is dangerous. It splits up the non-Byzantine mining power and slows down the longest chain growth. It leaves opportunities for Byzantines to canonicalize their controlled chain, and then to rewrite the history. In the case of multiple chain tips, peers are incentivized to mine on the longest chain. They can randomly choose to break the even. Consequently, once the network partition heals, mining power will quickly converge to the longest chain. For clients, they are advised to wait for their transactions to get buried in the longest chain deep enough. For example, six blocks behind the tip are often recommended. Assume that an asynchronous period, i.e., the network partition, will not last for 1 h. Then, a six-block fork is extremely unlikely to be a shorter one, given 10 min per block interval.

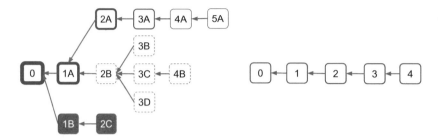

(a) Bitcoin's Longest-chain Rule in its Proof-of-Work   (b) Permissioned Blockchains' State-machine Repli-
Consensus   cation Consensus

Fig. 1.3 Comparison of ledger forks and canonical chain. The longest chain, as depicted in blue, in Bitcoin is considered canonical. Throughout, blocks at lower heights are more stable, as shown with their thicker borders. Red invalid blocks are out of the consensus consideration. Dashed blocks are unintentional chain forks, which may occur when peers are out of the sync. Permissioned blockchains, as later discussed in Chap. 1.3, adopt State-machine Replications (SMR) for the consensus. They prohibit any chain forks, as SMR provides instant finality

1.1.3   Bitcoin Versus Bank

Compared with traditional banking, Bitcoin provides the following benefits:

Decentralization. Decentralization lies at the very core of Bitcoin. Bitcoin, with PoW to mask Byzantines and reach consensus on payment history, eliminates any single point of failure. It also mitigates the stringent trust requirement on an authoritative intermediary. Decentralization makes it possible for anti-censorship, immutability, and other desirable security properties.

Anonymity. In Bitcoin, client identities are represented and hidden under asymmetric key pairs. In the common practice, clients locally generate a key pair. Then, they disseminate the public key hash as the recipient address. At last, they use the private-key-signed signatures to redeem the received amount. Throughout, the identity is not leaked. Key pairs are abundant. clients are recommended to use one-time addresses, to better preserve privacy. Peers can simply contribute their mining power to earn compensations. This can be done without their identities authenticated.

Sybil-resistant. Any anonymous system is vulnerable to Sybil Attacks. In a Sybil Attack, a malicious peer can generate a large number of identities, without any public awareness under the permissionless, unauthenticated setting. Then, the peer could make them act on its own behalf, so that the peer could amplify its system influence. PoW mitigates Sybil Attacks. In PoW, the weight of a peer consists in its contributing computational resources, rather than its possessed identities. In particular, a peer with a greater mining power, instead of more addresses, has a proportionally larger chance to mine a new block and get awarded. While identities are cheap to fake, computational power is difficult to attain. PoW thus makes a Sybil Attack prohibitively expensive.

Transparency. The complete transaction history, in the form of a ledger, is fully replicated in each blockchain peer. Without any access control, it is open to anyone. The ledger integrity is hash-chain-protected, so that clients may verify its validity. Furthermore, a transaction input references a previous transaction output. This structure enables tracking the cryptocurrency provenance to the minting event. In all, Bitcoin's transparency provides unprecedented auditability and accountability. This is far from comparable to any conventional banking system.

1.2 Ethereum Generalizes

Bitcoin uses decentralization to resolve the missing trust, without any single authoritative intermediary. However, the trust deficit not only plagues the application of monetary transfers, but it is also commonly seen in various sectors, like finance, supply chain, etc. Ethereum comes to the rescue—it generalizes the very promise of decentralization from Bitcoin; such that more sectors can take advantage of blockchain's trust-building capability.

1.2.1 Smart Contracts

For wider applicability, Ethereum made its debut in 2015. It introduces the revolutionary concept of *smart contracts*. A smart contract is a snippet of code that clients can deploy and invoke on the blockchain. A contract encodes a deterministic stateful transition. It resembles a function in programming languages, or a stored procedure in databases.

Thus, besides the normal cryptocurrency flow, Ethereum introduces two additional transaction types. We generally refer them as Deployment and Invocation transactions. Their transaction structure is much different from that in Bitcoin. Deployment transactions contain contract codes. They distribute contracts on each blockchain peer, with predefined logic and initial states. Contract deployment determines the identifier of a contract. Invocation transactions reference contract identifiers and provide parameters for the invocation. They initiate state transitions. Their execution and effects are replicated on each blockchain peer.

Listing 1.2 demonstrates an Ethereum, Solidity-coded contract that implements a counter. Its constructor, `Counter`, is auto-executed during deployment. It records down the address of its deployer to `admin`. This makes it possible for the contract to restrict the invocation of `incr_by_10` only to its deployer. In contrast, `incr_by_1` is accessible to the public. Let us compare it with the aforementioned Bitcoin script of a `pay-to-public-key-hash` transaction, shown in Listing 1.1. As one may observe, a smart contract allows for more customizations. While Bitcoin script operations are restricted to high-level cryptographic operations, a smart contract offers many low-level programming primitives such as loops, assignments, and computations. It empowers programmers to flexibly express their business logic, just like coding in any Turing-complete language. The contract's fine-grained access

```
OP_DUP  OP_HASH160  <Address>  OP_EQUAL  OP_CHECKSIG
```

Listing 1.1 Bitcoin's Pay-to-Public-Key-Hash Script. The script specifies that the later referencing transaction input must provide a public key matching the given hash(Address field) and provide a signature attesting for the possesstion of the corresponding private key

```
1      uint8 count;
2      address admin;
3
4      constructor() { admin = msg.sender; }
5
6      function incr_by_one() public { count+=1; }
7
8      function incr_by_ten() public {
9          require(msg.sender == admin);
10         count+=10;
11     }
12  }
```

Listing 1.2 An Ethereum's Smart Contract. It is coded in the Solidity programming language and implements a counter

control embodies another customization. This can be evidenced by the discriminated control on invokers of `incr_by_10` and `incr_by_one`. In sharp contrast, the Bitcoin script is entirely centered on cryptocurrency redemption rights. Apart from the above, smart contracts are stateful, while Bitcoin scripts are stateless. For example, `Counter` explicitly maintains `admin` address and `count`. The latter is subject to change for each Invocation transaction. On the other hand, a Bitcoin script is for one-time use. The output script becomes obsolete once the protected cryptocurrencies are redeemed.

1.2.2   Vulnerabilities and Mitigations

Statefulness and Turing-completeness of Ethereum offer unrivaled programmability for blockchain clients. But its contract-provided flexibility also comes with downsides. Under the mutually distrusting setup, these can be easily exploited by Byzantines. Below, we discuss several issues and mitigations.

Denial-of-the-service Attack and Gas Mechanism. A malicious client could deploy an exploitative contract. Its invocation would trigger an infinite loop. From the protocol, all peers are to replicate the execution and consequently hang in the loop. As we can see, this simple Denial-of-the-Service attack could bring the entire system to a halt. To disincentive such an action, the Ethereum protocol is equipped with the `Gas` management. This evolves from Bitcoin's transaction fee mechanism. Particularly, the protocol pre-associates each contract programming primitives with an amount of `gas`. Gas measures the execution complexity of the operations. The total gas of a transaction sums up from all operations in its contract call. It quantifies a transaction's computation complexity and overhead. Per each transaction, contract callers must also specify a gas price. The gas price specifies the number of cryptocurrencies per gas they are willing to pay. Then, the transaction fee can be calculated by multiplying its gas amount with its price. Similar to Bitcoin, contract callers credit the transaction fee to block proposers. In the above case, an infinite loop would translate into a run of countless operations. It would charge the caller an excessive amount of gas and transaction fees. Given this, a rational caller is incentivized to use services with care. The gas mechanism in Ethereum also encourages users to specify a higher gas price. It financially attracts block proposers to include their transactions earlier.

Statefulness and Synchronization While the total amount of Bitcoin is fixed, Ethereum-managed states can be arbitrarily large. It is no longer feasible for a ledger to encapsulate all of them. Instead, the Ethereum ledger only contains transactions. And each peer is expected to independently maintain the transaction effects in its own database. But, how can non-Byzantine peers be assured that they are synchronized on identical states? Likewise, how can clients be convinced that peers answer their state queries honestly? To address this problem, the Ethereum protocol additionally specifies the state organization format. This is as opposed to Bitcoin, which only mandates the ledger structure. In particular, each peer must organize states as a Merkle Patricia Trie (MPT) [42]. The tree-building procedure is deterministic and each tree node references children nodes with their hashes. States reside on leaf nodes such that the root hash uniquely identifies the encoded states. Then, the root can serve as the state digest. Under identical transactions and deterministic transitions, peers shall reach a common state; hence, their digests are expected to match. The Ethereum protocol mandates the digest as one of the block header fields so that the state-representing digest must undergo the consensus. In particular, after a peer receives a block proposal, it independently executes transactions and updates the MPT as the Ethereum protocol prescribes. The peer can then validate its self-computed root hash with the digest in the block header. The consistency is a part of the block legitimacy condition. If the majority agree on the digest, peers can be sure that they reach the same state. To answer a client's query on a state, the peers may attach the path from the Merkle tree root to the state leaf. This access path proves the validity of the result. Figure 1.4 illustrates an MPT with some details.

The explicit state maintenance with an MPT in Ethereum provides another benefit. It simplifies the transaction structure of normal cryptocurrency payments. An Ethereum transaction can be reduced to a bare-bone format, with a recipient address, a sender signature, and the transferred amount. This is as opposed to Bitcoin transactions, which must additionally enclose validation scripts and previous transaction references in their UTXO data model. The simplicity comes from the fact that the Ethereum protocol requires to directly book-keep addresses' balances in Externally Owned Accounts (EOV), a record entry in MPT. EOVs have no associated contract codes. They are simple associations of addresses and cryptocurrency balances. An address is computed from a public key and the private key controls the

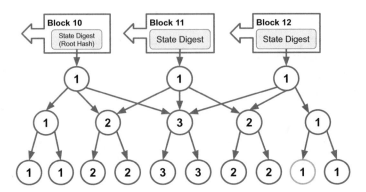

Fig. 1.4 The Merkle Tree in Ethereum. Ethereum states are organized as a Merkle Patricia Trie (MPT). Tree nodes, as illustrated in circles, are associated with their hashes in the storage, and children pointers are implemented as their hashes. The tree root hash is unique with respect to leaf states. Peers can use the root hash in the block header, as a digest for state synchronization. In addition, the content uniqueness of hash tries allows branches to be reused. The values in the illustrated tree nodes count how many times they are included in tries under Blocks 10, 11, or 12. Red tree path in Block 12 serves as the integrity proof for the state encoded in the orange leaf

monetary flow. The aforementioned contract scripts reside in Contract Accounts. Contract Accounts can also hold cryptocurrencies, but their transfers are under the governance of contract logics. As we will see in Sect. 4.1, custodial contracts play a vital role in Decentralized Finance.

1.3   Why Not Permissioned?

Ethereum retains the permissionless nature of Bitcoin, i.e., peers' identities are unknown, and they can join and leave the system at any time. However, in sectors other than cryptocurrencies, peers may be pre-authenticated. Their memberships are not subject to frequent churn. Consequently, Sybil-resistance is no longer required for the consensus. Hence, PoW becomes overkill due to its excessive energy consumption and limited performance.

In light of the above, system designers propose permissioned blockchains. They are specially tailored for enterprise usages with fixed and authenticated members. Their permissioned assumption allows a more efficient State-machine Replication (SMR), to achieve consensus and establish mutual trusts. Besides efficiency, SMR provides finality, i.e., no forks could occur in a ledger. Peers can be assured that blocks are unanimously decided, immediately when they are included in a ledger.

A number of permissioned systems leverage these authentication-provided benefits for the Byzantine-fault tolerant consensus. For example, Quorum [53] and Parity [47] are two popular source code forks of Ethereum. Both replace the original PoW consensus with IBFT and Proof-of-Authority, respectively. State-machine replication does not rely on peers' incentives to drive the procedure. Systems do not need an incentive mechanism to financially award non-Byzantine Peers; hence, permissioned blockchains can be cryptocurrency-free. Quorum and Parity retain most of the other features in Ethereum. These features include the contract deployment and invocation. The consensus modifications are transparent to users.

Beyond the consensus, well-established identities have the additional benefit of being accountable. As explained in Sect. 1.2.2, a fair charging plan is a prerequisite for contract-supported permissionless blockchains. It defers Denial-of-the-Service Attack from an anonymous attacker. The charging plan is on a basis of a standardized method to quantify a contract complexity. Inevitably, such standardization poses restrictions on allowable operations. Permissioned blockchains assume known identities and auditable actions. It relieves the concern for a strict, incentive-aligned behavior to deter anonymous attack. More operations can cater to a broader range of applications. For example, most business-targeted permissioned blockchains support private data. Private data refer to parts of transaction payloads and peer states which are visible to a selected set of peers. This is to support confidentiality, which is at the core of the business sector. Hyperledger Fabric and Quorum support private data. Besides, Corda [54] and Multi-chain [44] natively embed a number of well-developed financial primitives so that they can better streamline related services, without requiring users to develop them from scratch. The complexity of these high-level functionalities is hard to quantify; thus, they are not compatible with permissionless blockchains.

1.4   Summary and Further Reading

In this first chapter, we start from the ground-breaking Bitcoin, the very first decentralized blockchain system. As a cryptocurrency platform, we explain the constitution of the Bitcoin ledger, blocks, and transactions. We look into Bitcoin's transaction structure and UTXO data model, particularly how Bitcoin relies on asymmetric encryption for proof-of-ownership. We then delve into Bitcoin's soul, the Proof-of-Work (PoW) consensus protocol. PoW is a simple yet effective protocol for peers to reach an agreement on the ledger, given that a minority of them (the `Byzantines`) are non-compliant and the network delay is known upfront. PoW entails a continuous competition among peers to solve a hard-to-compute, easy-to-verify cryptographic puzzle (the `mining` process). A successful miner is rewarded with the privilege to broadcast a block and reaps mining and transaction fees. PoW achieves two-fold goals. First, it elevates the entry bar of block proposals, preventing Byzantines from flooding the system. Second, it controls the block generation interval to be greater than the network propagation delay. The margin minimizes the desynchronization periods due to in-transit blocks, and the peers can converge to an identical chain. Bitcoin's security features are highlighted by comparison to conventional banking systems.

Ethereum generalizes the decentralization idea of Bitcoin with smart contracts. Smart contracts support generic workloads with Turing-complete state transitions. With expanded utilities, smart contracts bring forward two security challenges. First, Turing-completeness

Table 1.1 Mainstream blockchains, their categories and domains

Blockchains	Authentication	Domain
Bitcoin [220]	Permissionless	Cryptocurrency
Litecoin [40]	Permissionless	Cryptocurrency
Ethereum [282]	Permissionless	General-purpose
Solana [287]	Permissionless	General-purpose
Quorum [53]	Permissioned	Business
R3 Corda [217]	Permissioned	Business
Hyperledger Fabric [91]	Permissioned	Business
Diem [61]	Permissioned	Finance
Ripple [94]	Permissioned	Finance

makes Denial-of-The-Service Attacks possible, by crafting an expensive contract call. This is mitigated by charging callers according to a protocol-prescribed payment plan and the transaction's complexity. Second, contract states can be too large to fit in the ledger. Peers must manage them locally and ensure global synchronization at the same time. To fix this issue, the Ethereum protocol mandates a deterministic data organization format (`Merkle Patricia Trie`). Peers with identical local states shall compute an identical digest. The digest is included in the block for peers to reach an agreement on their local states.

We motivate permissioned blockchains from the observation on many operating settings that their peers' identities are already known and authenticated. The authenticated setup relieves blockchain designers from the considerations of Sybil-resistance and incentives. This explains why permissioned blockchains have a strong penchant for State-machine Replication with Byzantine-tolerant consensus protocols. The smart contracts of permissioned blockchains are featured for enriched, high-level operations. This is opposed to permissionless Ethereum, whose contracts must be built upon low-level programming primitives. This is because low-level standardized primitives make it easier to quantify a contract's complexity. The ease of quantification makes possible a fair charging plan to incentivize against abused usages from anonymous users. In contrast, actions in permissioned blockchains are attributable and free of such concerns.

At last, Table 1.1 compiles existing popular blockchains with their permission nature and targeting domains. As one may observe, permissionless blockchains are either centered around cryptocurrencies or general-purpose if they support smart contracts. In contrast, permissioned blockchains are more tailor-made—they either dedicate to business or finance sectors. Interested readers may find more about these blockchains in Appendix A.2.

Blockchains and Distributed Databases

2

In the previous chapter, we start with Bitcoin. From Bitcoin, we draw out the evolution line of blockchains. Ethereum provides client-coded, Turing-complete smart contracts. It unleashes the decentralization potential of blockchains beyond cryptocurrencies. Furthermore, permissioned blockchains utilize the trusted membership setup in the operational setting. It makes it possible for efficient State-machine Replication and more flexible data operations.

From the recent-year progress, there is a clear trend that blockchains are getting closer to distributed databases. This is evidenced by their similar technical concepts. For example, blockchain smart contracts and databases' stored procedures both encode a state transition triggered by transactions. Both systems use consensus protocols for availability and robustness, and both require storage and indices for persistence and query.

Distributed database technologies are deeply interwoven in blockchains. Hence, the blockchain study naturally enters into the domain of data processing. Along this line, we re-examine blockchains from the lens of data processing systems. In particular, we propose a unified taxonomy that encompasses blockchains and distributed databases. In our framework, both systems fall into the category of distributed transactional platforms. Any of these platforms entails a fundamental performance-security trade-off, as shown in Fig. 2.1. Permissionless blockchains lie at the security end of the spectrum. Distributed databases are at the other performance end, while permissioned blockchains are situated in between. Along this principal axis, we systematically delineate their design choices at a finer grain. We organize our investigation on four dimensions as classified in the taxonomy. These four dimensions are Replication, Concurrency, Storage, and Sharding. At the end of this chapter, we apply our framework to analyze emerging hybrid systems. These hybrids are featured for the merging between blockchains and databases. Our framework lays out a common ground to analyze their security-performance trade-off. This chapter is inspired by our paper [247].

Fig. 2.1 Positions of blockchains and distributed databases on the performance-security spectrum. Permissionless blockchains lie at the security end of the spectrum, distributed databases at the other performance end, and permissioned blockchains in the middle

2.1   Why Blockchains and Databases?

In this part, we differentiate the use cases of blockchains and databases. Before that, let us refresh on database basics. Databases are software platforms that organize data for storage and query. Among all, relational databases, with application-friendly tabular data, intuitive SQL dialect, and handy ACID transaction semantics, remained dominant over decades. The recent demand for big data processing is pushing databases to scale out, as Moore's law has imposed a limit on the single-machine power. For higher availability and scalability, databases evolved to distribute data and computation over multiple computing nodes. Readers may refer to [228] for detailed techniques of distributed databases. Broadly, there are two distinct movements to scale out distributed databases, NoSQL and NewSQL.

For scalability, a few distributed databases move away from the ACID semantics and the traditional relational model. We refer to these systems as *NoSQL (Not-only SQL)*. NoSQL databases are accompanied by diverse data models, including key-value store (e.g., etcd [28], Redis [115]), document store (e.g., CouchDB [90]), graph store (e.g., Neo4J [273]), and column-oriented (e.g., Cassandra [185]). Another NoSQL aspect is that they no longer offer *linearizability*, i.e., reads must reflect the latest writes. Based on the CAP theorem [154], these NoSQL systems tilt toward availability and step away from consistency. On the other hand, *NewSQL* systems aim to retain the ACID semantics and the relational model despite their distributed setup. NewSQL started to gather momentum since Google's Spanner [128] debuted as the first NewSQL database. Some databases, such as CockroachDB [13] and TiDB [64], follow this trend. In our later comparison with blockchains, both NoSQL and NewSQL are considered.

As we can see, databases are created for data processing. Originally on a single node, the pressing scalability demand drives databases toward distributed settings. In contrast, blockchains are born with a distributed nature. Their targeting applications entail mutually distrusting parties. Each of them attempts to update a common data repository. But none of them is authoritative enough to convince others on the canonicity of its own managed data. And there is no external trusted intermediary for the remedy. Blockchains provide a distinctive trust-building capability to resolve conflicts and disputes. This capability is fundamentally powered by blockchains' Byzantine-fault tolerant consensus, such as PoW.

Table 2.1 Reported throughputs of blockchains and distributed databases

System	Category	Throughput (tps)
Bitcoin	Permissionless Blockchain	4.6 [190]
Ethereum	Permissionless Blockchain	15 [255]
Parity	Permissioned Blockchain	45 [138]
Quorum	Permissioned Blockchain	2.3k [232]
Hyperledger Fabric	Permissioned Blockchain	1k [267]
Redis	NoSQL Database	100k [80]
Etcd	NoSQL Database	50k [143]
TiDB	NewSQL Database	50k [81]

Though more blockchains now support smart contracts for generic workloads, the trust deficit, rather than data processing, remains to be a key driving force for the blockchain employment. Their distinction from databases is further evidenced below.

Firstly, there are several attempts to compare blockchains and distributed databases [125, 129, 283, 286]. Most of them provide an empirical flow chart to guide decisions per application demands. In their charts, one may observe that the missing trust and the lack of intermediaries are the topmost factors to consider for blockchains. Secondly, in terms of data processing speed, current blockchains are far from behind distributed databases. Their performance gap has long been identified, e.g., Bitcoin can process around 4.6 transactions per second (tps) [190] while etcd, which is a modern NoSQL database, can go up to over 50, 000 operations per second [143]. We compile more reported throughputs in Table 2.1. The large discrepancy comes as an acknowledgment that blockchain users could sacrifice performance for trustworthiness.

2.1.1 Why a Unified Taxonomy?

Many researchers are aware of the parallel between blockchains and distributed databases. Unfortunately, existing works fail to draw similarities between the two. They superficially conclude that blockchains are suitable for security-first applications, whereas databases fit scenarios where performance is the overarching concern. These existing comparisons barely scratch the surface: they restrict themselves to observable and measurable properties at the application-level, such as throughput, latency, and security. They stay short of digging further to account for the root causes. For example, BlockBench [138] compares three blockchains with a database. These blockchains are Fabric, Ethereum, and Parity, while the database is H-Store. Even though the authors expose the performance disparity, they provide no further analysis to make this disparity accountable. Apart from the workloads used in their experiments, these studies barely generalize.

To cross this chasm, we perform a comprehensive analysis of blockchains and databases, by placing them in the same design space, namely that of general transactional systems, based on higher abstraction levels. We introduce a taxonomy with four design dimensions. On this leveled playground, we discuss how blockchains and distributed databases diverge in their respective designs in each dimension. First, we consider the *replication* dimension, which deals with how and where to replicate data. It raises the challenge of replica synchronization. The second is *concurrency*, gauging the trade-offs between performance and concurrency-induced interference. The third dimension is *storage*, and it deals with the data abstraction and query methods. The fourth dimension is *sharding*: partitioning data to scale up. But sharding comes with tricky cross-shard transactions, especially when one needs to preserve atomicity.

The unified taxonomy not only helps understand both systems, but facilitate the reasoning of their hybrids as well. Lately, there is a growing importance of the trend of mixing databases and blockchains. In recent years, techniques from both systems are getting intermingled and their lines are blurring. For example, we have witnessed database concurrency control techniques used to speed up blockchains [134, 248, 260] and their hybrids [88]. At the same time, hybrid systems take advantage of security features inherited from blockchains to render verifiable storage services [88, 142, 233, 296]. These hybrid systems tend to mix different design choices and make their behavior hard to forecast. Our taxonomy provides a fair means to predict their performance and analyze their security.

2.2   Replication

Replication is a technique that copies data to nodes dubbed replicas. Spreading data to replicas provides multifaceted advantages. Clients can get faster data access from a near replica. Systems can continue to function as long as a set of replicas are responsive. Besides, maintaining more data copies scales up the system query volume.

Replication does not come with downsides. The key challenge in a replicated system is to ensure consistency. In particular, under a continuous stream of updates, how do replicas converge to common states? And such convergence must hold despite failures. Failures can take the form of crashed replicas, network partitions, and so on. On state convergence, researchers propose a series of consistency levels. These levels regulate the behavior of a replicated system, so that clients can reason about their effects. In this subsection, we characterize blockchains and distributed databases on replication. We focus on their replicated models, consistency levels, replication approaches, and failure models.

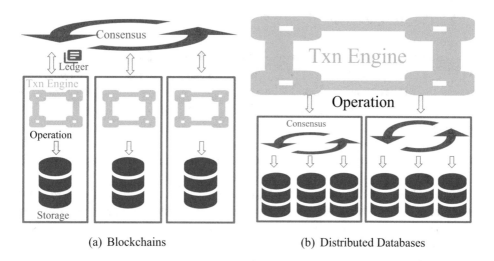

(a) Blockchains   (b) Distributed Databases

Fig. 2.2 Comparison of replications. **a** Blockchains first reach consensus on transactions and each node executes them independently. **b** Distributed databases have a central transaction component, which coordinates data operations. Data operations are replicated in the storage layer

2.2.1 Replication Model

Systems can perform replication at the granularity of transactions or the access operations that manipulate the storage. There are two elements to replicate on, one being to reach an agreement on transactions and the other to directly agree on the transactional effects, i.e., the modification on storage. The former approach induces more transparency by preserving high-level information, while the latter saves the storage overhead. Figure 2.2 shows that blockchains replicate a sequence of transactions, which are stored on the ledger. Each peer executes the transactions based on its local states in its own governed computing node. On the other hand, distributed databases replicate the storage operations. Database storage nodes are hence blind to the transaction details. Inevitably, the replication model in databases demands trust on the single-point transaction manager, a component that translates a transaction into storage operations and coordinates them. In contrast, blockchains are relieved from such security concerns. Blockchains eliminate any single point of failure—the entire transaction history is replicated and any participant peer can replicate its execution.

Replicating transactions in a ledger enables blockchains to preserve application-level information, such as the context of transactions, the signatures of the clients, and the execution timestamp, among others. This design facilitates participants to verify the transactions. Such verifiability is essential for blockchain to be used as a dispute-resolution platform for mutually distrusting parties. Replicating storage operations allows higher concurrency—replicated operations could be executed in any order as long as they achieve the same effect.

2.2.2 Consistency Level

A consistency level specifies rules on the allowable behavior of a replicated system. Fundamentally, it serves as a technique-oblivious agreement between systems and applications. The most notable consistency level is `Linearizable`. It mandates that reads must reflect the latest writes. Linearizability makes provisions to clients that replicated systems behave as a single replica.

In contrast, `Eventual Consistency` does not have such strict requirements. It only loosely calls for convergence, when there are no new data updates for a long time. In the middle, a number of other levels explore a variety of trade-offs.

Blockchains support Linearizable consistency level. Protocols mandate peers to follow the ledger-established transaction order for the execution. A block creating time determines the instants of its containing transactions. Hence, the ledger order respects the temporal sequence of transactions. A query proof must include a timestamp for clients' verification of the recency. As a consequence, their resulting effects exhibit Linearizability. NewSQL databases also stick to Linearizability. This is a part of the Consistency need in ACID transaction semantics. NoSQL offers a wider range of level choices. For example, Redis supports Linearizability. Cassandra [185], as another key-value storage, only guarantees Eventual Consistency.

2.2.3 Replication Approach

We are aware of two notable approaches to synchronize the replica. The first is *primary-backup*, and the second is *state-machine replication*. The primary-backup approach designates a fixed replica as the primary. The primary serves to synchronize its states with the backup replicas. Many databases employ this approach, such as Replex [265] and Cassandra [185]. State-machine replication keeps on each node (or replica) an ordered log of operations or transactions. Starting from the same initial state, each replica applies the operations or transactions in the agreed-upon sequence to converge to the identical state. Many systems employ *consensus protocols* to reach an agreement on the operation/transaction sequence. Protocols may range from Paxos [187], Raft [227], and to PBFT [118]. Example systems may include Quorum [53], TiDB [64], and Spanner [128]. One specialty of a consensus protocol versus the primary-backup is its automatic primary failover, by virtue of the view change. A view change kicks in when the consensus progress stalls. During this period, replicas work jointly to elect a new primary to continue driving the protocol. The crux of view change is to preserve the commit status of previous operations/transactions. Apart from the consensus, some systems outsource the implementation of distributed *shared log* abstraction to off-the-shelf external services. Example systems with outsourced shared log services include Fabric [37], Hyder [106], and Tango [101]. Kafka [39] and Corfu [100] are among a few popular shared log services.

Primary-backup protocols are more simple and they outperform state-machine replication especially when the states are of limited size and failures are of rare occurrence. For example, one of primary-backup protocols, named chain replication, can balance the network cost across replicas in a more even way compared to a consensus protocol. That is why it exhibits better read performance [265]. Shared log systems can be optimized for higher throughput by decoupling log ordering from state replication. It is well known that the performance (throughput and latency) of a consensus protocol worsens when more replicas are added to the system. The performance of a shared log system remains steady as long as the log consumers do not overwhelm the capacity of the log producers [100].

In all the above, replication is the system's internal behavior. In a sense, this is oblivious to clients. In contrast, leaderless replication leaves control to clients. Clients may, at their own discretion, contact subsets of replicas for data access. This flexibility allows clients to configure their own consistency levels. For example, consider the setting when a read and write replica set of clients overlaps. Then, one replica must be both accessed for query and update. Nonetheless, the replica will reply with the latest data. Likewise, clients can contact fewer replicas when the result recency is not a concern.

We observe almost all blockchains adopt consensus-based replication. So far, the only exception is Hyperledger Fabric [37]. It employs an external log producer, Kafka, to establish the transaction order and a ledger. Authors justify this design by the modularity consideration [91]. Primary-backup and state-machine replication are common in NewSQL, which targets Linearizability. All the above replication approaches can be found in some NoSQL databases. For example, Cassandra [185] employs leaderless replication for Eventual Consistency.

2.2.4   Failure Model

The complexity of replication protocols comes from the system faults they need to mask. Faults can be of different types and researchers come forward with failure models as abstractions to capture their differences. A protocol's failure model reflects its resilience against failures. The crash failure model assumes peers only fail by crashing (due to software or hardware problems). The protocols that support the crash failure model only need to tolerate such hardware and software faults. In the Byzantine failure model, peers are assumed to fail arbitrarily, including sending messages that deviate from the protocol to other peers. The corresponding protocols not only require to shield from aforementioned faults, but also to deter deliberate malicious behaviors from nodes. This model places the utmost concern on security since it takes into account arbitrary attacks that could sabotage the system.

The network assumption complements the above failure model by abstracting the network condition. The network is considered *synchronous* if the communication delay is explicitly known, and *asynchronous* otherwise. Like the failure model, the network assumption also impacts a protocol's resilience. Crash-fault tolerant (CFT) protocols require at least $f + 1$

nodes to tolerate f failures when the network is synchronous [112], and $2f + 1$ replicas when the network is asynchronous [187, 227]. Likewise, Byzantine-fault tolerant (BFT) protocols require $2f + 1$ and $3f + 1$ Replicas, respectively, under the synchronous and asynchronous networks [111, 118, 289].

Databases follow the crash failure model since expected-to-fail nodes are considered internal, centrally administrated. And hence, they do not consider nodes that behave arbitrarily. For example, Spanner [56] uses a CFT protocol called Paxos [186]. In contrast, permissioned blockchains come with a mixed preference of failure models. For example, Quorum allows users to select either Raft [227], a CFT protocol, or IBFT, a BFT protocol. In this way, the users will balance their desire for security and performance.

All permissionless blockchains, like Bitcoin, have no alternatives but BFT protocols due to their openness—any anonymous peers can join the system. Specifically, PoW-type of protocols are often favored because they overcome a key challenge in open and anonymous settings: identities are cheap to crank out such that a peer may control several identities to amplify its influence. In PoW-type of protocols, a peer's influence over the protocol and system is proportional to its hard-to-forge resources.

2.3   Concurrency

Concurrency is related to transactions. Though blockchains and databases independently define their transaction concepts, the fundamental is identical: a transaction is a logical group of data operations that satisfies certain properties. In particular, blockchain transactions refer mostly to ledger-included records, each of which encodes a smart contract invocation context. On the other hand, database transactions place more emphasis on the state transition properties. Concretely, the following four properties, with the acronym ACID, are the default in most traditional databases.

Atomicity. Operations in a transaction shall take effect in the entirety.

Consistency. A transaction shall preserve application-defined invariants.

Isolation. Concurrent transactions shall not interfere with each other.

Durability. Transaction effects shall survive hardware failures and software faults.

Transactions, by providing the above guarantees, reduce the efforts of database users. For example, a bank user is free from the concern on the potential halfway effects of a monetary transfer.

Concurrency pertains to the Isolation property. As opposed to the other three properties, Isolation is vague on the `interference`. And this is what concurrency gauges on. Concurrency specifies rules to define correctness conditions on allowable concurrency-induced anomalies. There is a hierarchy of isolation levels [99], each with its own rules. More rules imply more sequential restrictions and fewer speedup opportunities. The most intuitive level is *Serializable*. It dictates the resulting effects of transactions must be equivalent to one of their serialized plans. As its name implies, a literal sequential execution satisfies the Seri-

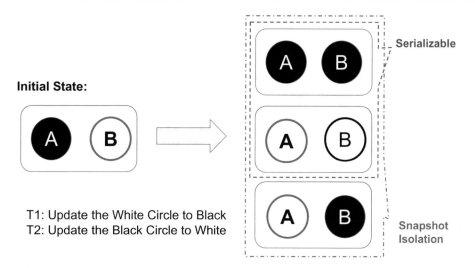

Fig. 2.3 Comparison of Serializable and Snapshot Isolation levels, with an example adapted from [11]. An initial state consists of black Circle A and white Circle B. Two transactions T1 and T2 attempt to flip the color of white and black circles, respectively. Serializable only permits a total of two scenarios where both circles share the same color, as enclosed by the blue dashed-border box. The both-white (both-black) scenario corresponds to T1-first, T2-second (T2-first, T1-second) transaction plan. Snapshot Isolation allows a third possibility, where two circles' colors are flipped. It is because T1 and T2 can start simultaneously, not aware of each other. Both select distinct circles to update and hence both get committed due to no conflicts. Three Snapshot Isolation-allowed possibilities are enclosed by the red dashed-border box

alizable level. Some sophisticated concurrent approaches are also available. For example, two-phase lock (2PL) uses locks to protect common data access across transactions. As opposed to Serializable, *Snapshot Isolation* makes the following specifications. Queries in transactions must be answered by the latest state before transactions start, and a transaction can make an effect if its updated records are not concurrently modified by others. As illustrated in Fig. 2.3, Snapshot Isolation allows for more result possibilities. As a more lenient isolation level, Snapshot Isolation is more concurrency-friendly than Serializable.

Isolation levels are abstractions that regulate the intertransaction interference. They are implementation-oblivious. We generally classify them into two categories based on their implementation choices. That is, the transactions are executed (i) serially or sequentially, one after another, or (i) they are executed concurrently. Most blockchains embrace serial execution, a literal way to implement Serializable level. In contrast, distributed databases attempt to extract as much concurrency as the isolation level allows.

Several reasons are behind the blockchains' tepidity toward concurrency, especially for permissionless blockchains. The performance bottleneck of permissionless blockchains is the consensus, which would dwarf any speedup that concurrency could bring. For example, the Bitcoin consensus protocol dictates blocks to be generated at a fixed interval of 10 min. In contrast, the serial execution of internal transactions, which runs the Bitcoin script to redeem cryptocurrencies, can finish within a second. Next, sequentiality implies the deterministic nature of smart contract behaviors, when individual peers replicate the contract execution. The determinism facilitates peers to reason about their behavior and verify the system states.

Unlike blockchains, concurrency remains at the center of database research and the focus of NewSQL databases. Nowadays, most production-grade databases provide a multitude of isolation levels for operators to balance the concurrency and execution correctness. To implement isolation levels, database techniques can belong to either of the pessimistic and optimistic approaches. The former, such as 2PL, regulates the transaction interference with locks or mutexes. And the latter assumes data conflicts are rare. Systems run transactions on a best-effort basis, except for a clear sign of intolerable anomalies.

Transactions have offered tremendous utilities. Despite this, transactions fall victim to the recent NoSQL movement. Some NoSQL advocates blame transactions for issues with scalability and availability. This is in line with the design of some NoSQL systems. They completely abandon transaction restrictions. Instead, they place more focus on concurrent, scalable, and available designs. For example, many NoSQL databases partition data into multiple shards so that concurrency is favored for intra-shard operations. But they no longer make any guarantee on the cross-shard operations. This may pose difficulties for applications.

2.4   Storage

Storage preserves states despite system failures. As an indispensable component, storage is the key enabler for transaction durability. It organizes data onto hardware devices so that states can survive hardware faults and software crashes. Besides persistence, data organization must also facilitate data queries. We refer to a data organization as `index`. In this section, we look inside blockchains and distributed databases, dissecting their storage. Particularly, we look at storage models, i.e., what they persist, and indices, i.e., how they organize data.

2.4.1   Storage Model

Storage can be oriented toward the frequently mutated latest states or append-only historical information. The conventional databases opt for the former, by providing access to the latest, up-to-date records. In databases, there are some historical data but in limited forms, e.g., write-ahead logs. Such logs serve for failure recovery and are usually pruned from time to time. In contrast, blockchains manage both the latest states and historical information. The ledger, which is a defining feature of blockchains, dictates systems to record all historical transactions and their manipulations on the global states. Notably, the ledger is protected by cryptographic hashes to preserve the historical integrity.

2.4.2 State Organization

The data organizations, represented by indices, are vital for the data access on state storage. Apart from the performance, indices can be hung on to compute a digest in order to identify a certain state of the database in a unique way. Distributed databases focus more on the performance aspect. The storage access frequency could magnify any tiny index optimization to an appreciable improvement on system efficiency. This explains a prominent trend in database research where indices often come forward with their tailored hardware. The index design can push the hardware to the limit to achieve utmost efficiency. For instance, two indices are ingrained into the architecture of on-disk databases, namely B-tree and LSM tree. The former can be regarded as a binary tree with multiple fan-outs. A tree node is configured to fit into a disk page, the basic data unit of a magnetic drive. B-trees reduce scattered data access for better locality. On the other hand, LSM trees are tailored for the append-only nature of disk drives. In LSM trees, all data updates, including modifications and removals, take in the form of append operations. Background processes periodically perform compactions, which override earlier operations with later ones. As opposed to employing the above disk-friendly indexes, in-memory databases turn for FAST [175] and PSL [285]. These indices target multi-core parallelism and better CPU cache utilization.

For the computation of the content-unique digest, blockchains organize the state storage into an authenticated data structure. Popular structures in blockchains are all variants of a Merkle tree. As an example, Ethereum utilizes a prefix trie known as Merkle Patricia Trie (MPT) [42]. As we explained in Sect. 1.2.2, the states reside in the MPT leaves. Moreover, the states having a common prefix in their keys are arranged under the same tree branch. A flat storage engine associates each tree node with its cryptographic hash. As such, the root hash uniquely represents the encapsulated system states. The path to access a leaf amounts to the proof of integrity for the queried value. Fabric 0.6, an older version of Hyperledger Fabric, uses a Merkle Bucket Tree (MBT). Unlike MPT, the number of MBT's leaves, the buckets, are fixed. States are hashed into buckets and a Merkle tree is built on top of bucket hashes. Figure 2.4 illustrates their differences with example data.

2.5 Sharding

Sharding partitions data into disjoint shards to concurrently manage them. The database community has extensively studied this technique as a way to scalability. Blockchains are born without sharding—the ledger in Bitcoin is fully replicated in each peer. However, blockchain designers have been increasingly aware of sharding to harness their brought-up concurrency across shards (Fig. 2.5). Below we discuss two problems that handicap any sharded systems—shard formation and the cross-shard transaction atomicity.

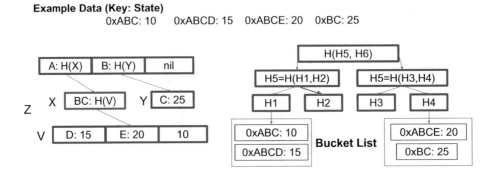

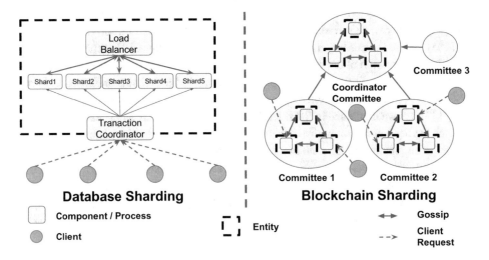

Fig. 2.4 Comparison of Merkle Patricia Trie (MPT) and Merkle Bucket Tree (MBT). Ethereum and Ethereum-forked systems employ MPT, while Hyperledger Fabric v0.6 employs MBT. Both MPT and MBT are Merkle tree variants, i.e., tree node pointers are implemented as hashes. MBT is built upon data buckets, while MPT organizes records based on key prefixes. A red MPT node may compress the common prefix path in keys

Fig. 2.5 Comparison of sharding in blockchain and distributed databases. In distributed databases, there exists a central transaction coordinator that coordinates shard access via 2PC. There may be a load balancer to adjust shard assignments based on workloads. Shards in blockchains are organized in peer committees. There may be a coordinator committee, which assumes the similar duty of a database coordinator

2.5.1 Shard Formation

Shard formation concerns the distribution of data and nodes/peers to shards. Such distribution is vital for blockchains—their security is based on the assumption of a bounded number of failures. Consequently, the shard formation must make sure that this assumption stays true for every shard. As such, the size of the shard has to be big enough to bound the fraction of Byzantine peers to a tolerable limit. Furthermore, attackers must be deterred from influencing the shard assignment; otherwise, they could concentrate on a single shard to break through the entire defense. In permissionless blockchains, shard formation protocols must be additionally secured against Sybil attacks. Blockchains also conduct shard reconfiguration periodically to protect against adaptive attackers. State-of-the-art sharded blockchains employ different methods to mitigate the above issues. We will analyze the state of the arts in the next chapter.

Sharding in distributed databases aims to scale up performance. The shard formation scheme is closely tied up to the nature of workloads. In practice, we observe that database vendors offer a variety of partitioning schemes, so that clients can choose the most suitable to fit their workloads. For example, there are two notable partitioning schemes, namely hash partitioning and range partitioning. The former can spread out workloads evenly but is not amenable to range queries. The latter scheme serves the opposite. Some systems, such as Cassandra [185], enable the partitioning of data in a locality-aware manner. Different from blockchains, databases do not demand shard reconfigurations.

2.5.2 Cross-Shard Transactions

Sharding exaggerates the atomicity problem when a transaction spans numerous shards. Atomicity stipulates that a cross-shard transaction should produce effects in its entirety, which is either commit or abort the effects in all the involved shards. Nowadays, the golden standard in distributed databases is the two-phase commit (2PC) protocol. This protocol designates a coordinator to drive the protocol. But the coordinator must be trusted; its failure would block the progress.

The excessive trust in the single-point coordinator makes 2PC incompatible with sharded blockchains. A naive solution would be to harden 2PC against Byzantine attacks. Along with this spirit, some sharded blockchains implement the 2PC coordinator on a group of peers that runs a BFT protocol [133]. In particular, the consensus of peers secures the 2PC state transitions. The liveness of the BFT consensus protocol guarantees the availability of the coordinator, thus solving the blocking problem. Inevitably, such idiomatic composition between 2PC and BFT protocols incurs considerable overheads. As we will see in Sect. 3.4.3, several researchers explore pairing 2PC and BFT protocols more judiciously or letting clients take the coordinator role.

2.6   Benchmarking

From our above taxonomy-guided classification, blockchains are but a category of distributed transactional systems, sharing abundant similarities with distributed databases. Given this, it shall come as no surprise that many researchers put both systems in a leveled playground for benchmarking, e.g., both evaluated under database workloads. Simple as it may be, porting database workloads to blockchains is not a trivial task, due to the fundamental difference in the transaction processing nature of the two system categories. In this subsection, we first lay out the design differences of respective benchmarking frameworks, before walking through several renowned benchmarking results.

2.6.1   Benchmarking Frameworks

Database benchmarking frameworks are closed-loop (or blocking), while those for blockchains are open-loop (or non-blocking). Concretely, in the former, each working thread submits a transaction, waits for its completion, and records its status (committed/aborted) before sending the next transaction. In contrast, the blockchain's open-loop thread submits a transaction and immediately returns with its transaction identifier. A separate status thread polls the target blockchain with the collected transaction identifiers for their corresponding status. Figure 2.6 compares the two benchmarking modes visually. Such disparity can be eas-

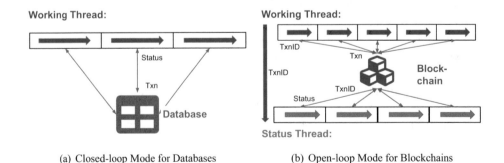

(a) Closed-loop Mode for Databases   (b) Open-loop Mode for Blockchains

Fig. 2.6 Distinction between the two benchmarking framework modes. In the closed-loop mode, a working thread submits a transaction to the target database and waits for its finishing status before sending subsequent ones. In the open-loop mode, the thread submits a transaction and immediately returns with its transaction identifier. A separate status thread polls the target blockchain with transaction identifiers collected from working threads for their status

ily accounted for by the difference in transaction processing nature between blockchains and databases. Databases are synchronous: transactions from a client connection are immediately processed in a first-come-first-serve way. In contrast, blockchains process transactions in an asynchronous mode: arrived transactions are first buffered in a pool, undergo validation, and get selectively picked for execution, i.e., being batched into a block for the consensus. In this manner, consider we mount a blocking framework to a blockchain. If a transaction does not pass through the validation (e.g., another committed transaction modifies the system state with respect to which this transaction is no longer valid), this transaction's issuing client will get forever blocked. Or it will wait for a lengthy timeout, significantly delaying subsequent transactions' submission. In contrast, an open-loop framework does not suffer this problem—a separate status thread will conclude the timeout. Given the prompt firing rate, an open-loop mode needs fewer running threads to throttle the system, compared to a closed-loop one.

Popular open-loop benchmarking frameworks for blockchains include BlockBench [138] and Caliper [10], while closed-loop benchmarking frameworks for databases abound— YCSB [127], OLTPBench [135], HammerDB [36], SysBench [59], and those suites coming along with specific databases [65]. In terms of workloads, the key-values of YCSB [127], Smallbank [114], and TPC-C [68] are widely accepted for database benchmarking. In contrast, those for blockchains are lacking standards—many evaluations either directly port database workloads [138, 247] or rely on proprietary datasets [267].

2.6.2   Benchmarking Reports

In the BlockBench paper, the authors propose the first-ever benchmarking framework for permissioned blockchains, and they apply it to three permissioned blockchains, namely Hyperledger Fabric v0.6, Parity, and Ethereum [138]. Comparing these blockchains with a database, namely H-Store, the conclusion is as expected: the performance of blockchains lags behind databases under database workloads. However, given the magnitude-level disparity, researchers believe such a gap shall not be solely attributed to the blockchain's excessive emphasis on security. This mystery is partly solved in [247], where researchers perform a much finer-grained benchmarking with respect to individual layers in the aforementioned taxonomy. By pining down layer-wise effects on the system behavior, this work sheds light on the performance disparity between the two system categories. The in-depth understanding allows for a better forecast of the system behavior beyond database workloads. References [198, 199] complement BlockBench by evaluating the energy consumption of permissioned blockchains. In addition to traditional servers with x86/64 architecture, these works analyze emerging servers with 64-bit ARM processors. Reference [151] extends the benchmarking to the later-mentioned fusions of blockchain-database systems. Besides the aforementioned works, there is a variety of blockchain evaluations in the academic literature. For completeness, we tabulate some of these works in Table 2.2 according to their target blockchain.

Table 2.2 Blockchain benchmarking reports

Platform	References
Hyperledger Fabric	[138, 198, 221, 234, 247, 267, 269]
Ethereum	[121, 138, 198, 234, 245]
Quorum	[102, 247]
Parity	[138, 198]
Corda	[79, 269]

2.7 Fusion

In recent years, we observe the trend of mixing blockchain and database techniques into hybrid blockchain-database systems. Here, we analyze these systems via our proposed taxonomy. We can broadly classify these systems into two main categories.

Out-of-the-blockchain Databases. These are systems that start from a blockchain, or a system with blockchain features, and build a database on top of it. For example, BlockchainDB [142] and FalconDB [233] build shared, verifiable databases with blockchain properties for distrusting organizations.

BlockchainDB, depicted in Fig. 2.7, replicates storage operations and uses full-fledged blockchains at the storage layer. Moreover, BlockchainDB supports multiple blockchains at the same time by adopting the sharding technique. BlockchainDB inherits the ledger structure, which is an authenticated data structure that provides immutability, from the underlying blockchains.

Borrowing the idea from the lightning network [236], FalconDB enables verification by lightweight clients which do not have the full copy of the states. FalconDB uses Tendermint [111] for consensus and a similar optimistic concurrency control as Hyperledger Fabric. For providing proofs and verifying the integrity of the data, FalconDB uses IntegriDB [298]. This allows lightweight peers to produce integrity proofs without keeping the entire ledger.

Out-of-the-database Blockchains. The other design approach starts from a database system and adds blockchain technologies on top of it. Such examples of hybrid out-of-the-database blockchains are Veritas [88], BigchainDB [207], Blockchain Relational Database (BRD) [222], and ChainifyDB [256]. These systems consist of peers that maintain local databases on top of which they execute transactions based on a global order. This global order is achieved through a form of consensus. Then, the ledger is used to preserve this global order of transactions. As such, these systems employ a replication model at the transaction-level. Each peer in the system executes the transactions in the same order, but on a different local database. It is possible to have different types of databases in different nodes. In such a case, the ledger on each peer saves the transactions in its database vendor-specific format. This is different from blockchains. For example, Quorum embeds LevelDB as a slim storage component and runs it in the same process. Going back to the above out-of-the-

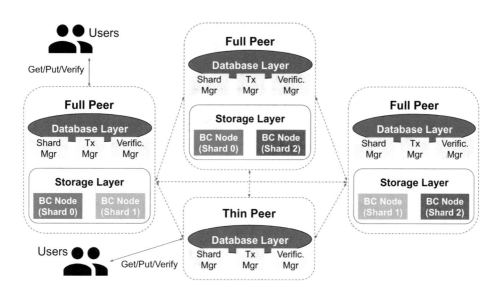

Fig. 2.7 The design of BlockchainDB, a hybrid blockchain-database system. Each full peer maintains both (1) a database layer to provide data access to users and (2) a storage layer built on top of blockchains. A peer may use multiple, different blockchains at the storage layer, supporting sharding. Thin peers only provide a database layer to users and rely on full peers for access to the storage

database blockchains, Veritas keeps Redis key-value update operations in the Kafka shared log. BigchainDB uses MongoDB [43], and the transactions are in a JSON format. BRD uses PostgreSQL [264] and a transaction embeds the invocation context of the stored PostgreSQL procedures. In ChainifyDB, the transaction is kept as standardized SQL statements. Veritas and ChainifyDB use the Apache Kafka broadcasting service to keep transaction logs. Kafka is a CFT system with high efficiency. On the other hand, BigchainDB uses Tendermint, which is a BFT consensus protocol. BRD employs both Kafka [39] and BFT-SMaRt [107], which is an extension of the PBFT consensus protocol. At the storage level, these out-of-the-database blockchains inherit the performance improvements of their underlying databases, but the transactions are executed sequentially following the ledger order.

Next, we analyze Veritas, as depicted in Fig. 2.8. Veritas provides a shared database or a shared table across distrusting organizations. To keep track of the changes to this shared database, an external broadcasting service and a ledger are used. In its original design, both the broadcasting service and the ledger are implemented with Apache Kafka, a CFT system. This original design of Veritas was modified [151] to incorporate BFT consensus protocols such as Tendermint [111] and HotStuff [289]. Moreover, the modified open-source version [88] of Veritas implements the ledger with a Sparse Merkle Tree [130], thus, providing additional data integrity and auditability.

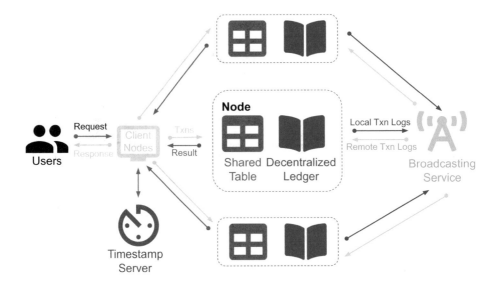

Fig. 2.8 The design of veritas, a hybrid blockchain-database system. Each node maintains the shared database/table and a ledger. The ledger keeps track of the changes done to the shared table. Queries are served directly by the nodes, while updates are first broadcasted to all the nodes and persisted only if acknowledged by a majority of the nodes. We classify Veritas as an out-of-the-blockchain database

In conclusion, out-of-the-database blockchains are closer to distributed databases, where the key goal is performance. This is in contrast to out-of-the-blockchain databases which focus more on security by using more techniques from blockchains. Nonetheless, we also note the recent trend of centralized, cloud-based verifiable databases, such as Alibaba LedgerDB [288], Amazon QLDB [5], LedgeBase [291], and Spitz [296]. These systems use the hashed-link ledger data structures and authenticated data structures from blockchains, but do not employ BFT consensus protocols. Other systems, such as LogBase [271], provide custom optimizations on the ledger data structure.

2.8   Summary and Further Reading

This chapter draws a general comparison between blockchains and distributed databases. The comparison presents a distinctive angle, uniquely tailored for database people, for a better understanding of blockchains. We start from the gaps in existing works. Current researchers restrict their focus on systems' application-level differences. Instead, our taxonomy, by unifying blockchains and distributed databases under a distributed transactional platform, provides a comprehensive description of their internal design spaces.

Table 2.3 A compilation of distributed transactional systems based on our taxonomy. For each hybrid system, we mark their security-oriented designs with red and performance-oriented designs with blue. This table is taken from [247]

Category	System	Replication			Concurrency	Storage		Sharding Support (2PC)
		Replication Model	Replication Approach	Failure Model (Consensus Protocol)		Ledger Abstraction	Index(Storage Engine)	
Permissionless Blockchains	Ethereum [29]	Txn-based	Consensus	BFT(PoW)	Serial	✓	LSM Tree(LevelDB)+MPT	✗(✗)
	Eth2 [30]	Txn-based	Consensus	BFT(PoS + Casper)	Serial (in each shard)	✓	LSM Tree(LevelDB)+MPT	✓(✗)
Permissioned Blockchains	Quorum v2.2 [53]	Txn-based	Consensus	Raft(CFT)/IBFT(BFT)	Serial	✓	LSM Tree(LevelDB)+MPT	✗(✗)
	Fabric v2.2 [37]	Txn-based	Shared log	CFT(*Orderer* with Raft)	Concurrent Execution Serial Commit	✓	LSM Tree(LevelDB)	✗(✗)
	Fabric v0.6 [34]	Txn-based	Consensus	BFT(PBFT)	Serial	✓	LSM Tree(RocksDB) + MBT	✗(✗)
	EOS [25]	Txn-based	Consensus	BFT(DPoS)	Serial	✓	B-tree(MongoDB)	✗(✗)
	FISCO BCOS [35]	Txn-based	Consensus	CFT(Raft) BFT(PBFT)	Serial	✓	LSM Tree(LevelDB) +MPT	✗(✗)

(continued)

Table 2.3 (continued)

Category	System	Replication			Concurrency	Storage		Sharding Support (2PC)
		Replication Model	Replication Approach	Failure Model (Consensus Protocol)		Ledger Abstraction	Index(Storage Engine)	
NewSQL Databases	TiDB v4.0 [64]	Storage-based	Consensus	CFT(Raft)	Concurrent	✗	LSM Tree(TiKV)	✓(✓)
	CockroachDB [13]	Storage-based	Consensus	CFT(Raft)	Concurrent	✗	LSM Tree(RocksDB)	✓(✓)
	Spanner [56]	Storage-based	Consensus	CFT(Paxos)	Concurrent	✗	LSM Tree	✓(✓)
	H-store [172]	Storage-based	Primary-backup	CFT	Concurrent	✗	B Tree	✓(✓)
NoSQL Databases	Etcd v3.3 [28]	Storage-based	Consensus	CFT(Raft)	Serial	✗	B Tree(BoltDB)	✗(✗)
	Cassandra [12]	Storage-based	Primary-backup	CFT	Concurrent	✗	LSM Tree	✓(✗)
	DynamoDB [4]	Storage-based	Primary-backup	CFT	Concurrent	✗	B Tree	✓(✗)
Out-of-the Blockchain Databases	BlockchainDB [142]	Storage-based	Consensus	BFT(PoW)	Serial (in each shard)	✓	LSM Tree(LevelDB)+MPT	✓(✗)
	Veritas [88]	Storage-based	Shared log	CFT(Kafka)	Concurrent Execution Serial Commit	✓	Skip List(Redis)	✗(✗)
	FalconDB [233]	Storage-based	Consensus	BFT(Tendermint)	Concurrent Execution Serial Commit	✓	B Tree(MySQL)+Merkle Tree(IntegriDB)	✗(✗)
Out-of-the Database Blockchains	Blockchain Relational Database (BRD) [222]	Txn-based	Shared log	CFT(Kafka) BFT(BFT-SMaRt)	Concurrent	✓	B Tree(PostgreSQL)	✗(✗)
	ChainifyDB [256]	Txn-based	Shared log	CFT(Kafka)	Concurrent	✓	B Tree (MySQL/PostgreSQL)	✗(✗)
	BigchainDB [207]	Txn-based	Consensus	BFT(Tendermint)	Concurrent	✓	B Tree(MongoDB)	✗(✗)

At the end of this chapter, we demonstrate our taxonomy's utility by applying it to reason about recent blockchain-database fusions. Besides the above hybrid systems, Table 2.3 taken from our previous work [247] summarizes a wider range of representative transactional systems. Table 2.3 only considers contract-supporting blockchains and key-value NoSQL databases. We use our taxonomy to summarize the design choices of these systems. We observe that the hybrid systems as well as permissioned blockchains come with a mixed flavor on security-oriented designs expected of blockchains and performance-oriented designs expected of databases.

At last, curious readers may doubt that blockchains are very similar to peer-to-peer databases [272]. Both are decentralized—nodes are administrated by loosely knitted individuals. They are facing similar threats and seeing shared mitigation techniques, e.g., they both employ Merkle trees to protect the data integrity. Moreover, these superficial similarities never obscure their following glaring distinction. Blockchains call for a strong notion of consensus, due to the presence of a ledger. All transactions, even though they are touching a disjoint set of records, must be totally ordered. In contrast, peer-to-peer databases manage records and files independently. They are less concerned about operations that span multiple data items.

In all, this chapter aims to guide readers into blockchains with the help of more familiar database concepts. We would recommend these tutorials to readers keen to dig deeper into their intersections [214–216].

Blockchain State of the Art

3

In the previous chapter, we examine the many similarities between blockchains and distributed databases, and discuss how blockchains prioritize security and robustness over performance. The important research questions concerning blockchains are (1) how they strengthen robustness, and (2) how they improve performance without impacting security.

In this chapter, we review the latest progress on answering these two questions. We structure our discussion according to the taxonomy defined in Chap. 2, and provide in-depth details on the theories, techniques, and the systems.

3.1 Replication

Replication spreads data into replicas for fault tolerance, locality, and workload balancing. It brings challenges to data synchronization under frequent updates, network partitions, or node crashes. Blockchains employ replication to distribute the transactions and the decentralized ledger to nodes. Then, mutually distrusted peers independently execute the transactions. As shown in Sect. 2.2.3, there are a few approaches to achieve replication. Despite this, we observe that most blockchains rely on consensus, instead of primary-backup. Hence, we mostly target state-of-the-art consensus-based approaches in blockchains. Firstly, we focus on the formal analysis on Proof-of-Work (PoW). We show how researchers reduce PoW to a Byzantine-fault tolerant protocol, and study how they evolve mathematical models to strengthen Bitcoin's robustness reasoning. Afterward, we investigate several approaches to enhance PoW. Notable directions are making PoW faster, usable, and greener. At last, we review the recent progress on the Byzantine-fault tolerant state-machine replication.

3.1.1 Proof-of-Work and Analysis

PoW underpins Bitcoin's security. Concretely, the non-Byzantine majority is assumed to extend on the longest chain. Then, the growth of the longest chain outpaces other alternatives so that it remains the longest. Clients can be assured about the chain stability. The peers reach consensus on committed transactions, despite Byzantines' arbitrary manipulation. This Byzantine-fault tolerant guarantee is heuristically shown in the Bitcoin whitepaper [220]. In particular, the probability of toggling the longest chain drops off exponential with Z, where Z is the block distance which a Byzantine-controlled, shorter chain aims to catch up. However, the security reasoning of Nakamoto is over-simplified and lacking formalism. One oversimplification is the overlook of certain realistic conditions. These conditions may pose non-negligible effects on the security, i.e., the longest chain stability. The lack of formalism can be evidenced by the underestimates of Byzantines' behavior. In particular, Nakamoto assumes Byzantines immediately publish a mined block. However, further studies show that such an immediate-broadcast policy may not be optimal for their best interest. Below, we outline the recent progress on the security analysis of PoW and related protocols. One line of effort lies in the establishment and evolution of formalism. And the other is on the mining policy study, i.e., how Byzantines and non-Byzantine peers are incentivized to behave.

Security Modeling. Fundamentally, PoW is a protocol that addresses Byzantine-fault tolerance, which is a classic problem in Distributed Computing. In the problem setting, there is a network and a set of processes. Each process has an initial value to propose. The processes exchange messages and make state transitions, according to a protocol specification. The consensus protocol is defined as Byzantine-fault tolerant as follows. Given Byzantine processes do not exceed a threshold fraction f, the following properties hold:

1. **Safety.** All non-Byzantine processes decide on the same value.
2. **Liveness.** All non-Byzantine processes will decide in a finite time.
3. **Validity.** The decided value must be the proposed value of a non-Byzantine process and satisfies application-specific predicates.

Based on the nature of the network, a Byzantine-fault tolerant consensus protocol can be further broken down into `synchronous` and `asynchronous`. The former assumes the network delay and the process computing speed are known and bounded. Hence, processes are allowed to use timeouts to reason about others' status. The latter does not have this assumption, as the network is assumed to reorder or lose messages arbitrarily. But delayed messages are eventually delivered. An asynchronous network captures the scenario where the network is within the control of Byzantines.

Nakamoto employs PoW to solve the Byzantine consensus problem in the cryptocurrency domain. For wider applicability, [212] abstracts a generic, probabilistic protocol out of Bitcoin. Researchers prove that, with high probability, the abstracted protocol solves the above Byzantine-fault tolerant problem. This is under the synchronous network and Byzantine threshold $f < 1/2$, and Bitcoin is one of the protocol instantiations. Particularly, **Safety** and **Liveness** take the respective form of longest chain stability and growth. The legitimate conditions of ledgers, blocks, and transactions embody the application-specific predicates, as demanded by **Validity**.

While the above marks an initial attempt to reduce PoW into an existing, well-defined problem, [150] aims to reformulate the consensus problem to specifically tailor it for blockchains. Researchers put forth the Bitcoin backbone protocol with two fundamental properties. Two properties are **Common Prefix** and **Chain Quality**. **Common Prefix** specifies how many common blocks two peers share in their committed ledger. It is the **Safety** counterpart with respect to the traditional definition. Likewise, as the **Validity** counterpart, **Chain Quality** specifies the ratio of Byzantine-proposed blocks. With the Bitcoin backbone protocol, researchers prove and reduce the Byzantine threshold f from $1/2$ to $1/3$ [150]. This result is consistent with the later-mentioned Selfish Mining Policy [146]. As a carry-on work, [173] complements the Bitcoin backbone protocol with a new property called **Chain Growth**. **Chain Growth** essentially corresponds to **Liveness**. Reference [173] further demonstrates the utility of the augmented backbone protocol by applying it on Ghost [263], another PoW protocol. All above models assume synchrony, where the network and processing delay bound is exposed to protocols. Reference [229] lifts up the assumption on synchrony. The authors propose their own abstract notion of a blockchain protocol with the asynchronous setting. In addition, their model accounts for the dynamic membership changes. Non-fixed membership is a realistic assumption for permissionless blockchains. Reference [174] tightens the **Safety**-related properties, by a novel method powered by Markov chains. This is opposed to traditional approaches which model the mining procedure as a Poisson process. In a similar fashion, researchers extend their Markov-chain-powered model to reason about Ghost [263] and CliqueChain [206]. At last, the analysis in [241] is featured for its simplicity.

Mining Strategy. There has long been a misperception of the optimality of the default mining policy—peers mine on the longest chain and immediately broadcast a block once discovering a valid nonce. Conventional wisdom believes in the fairness of the default policy. Peers earn rewards in proportion to their computing resources, despite their arbitrary behavior. However, Self-Mining policy [146] smashed this wrong illusion. This new policy plays with Bitcoin's forking mechanism, enabling participants with a competitive edge in the block mining competition. It is mounted as follows, and a concrete example can be later found in Fig. 3.1a. Instead of immediate broadcast, attackers withhold the discovered blocks and continue to mine on top. The withheld blocks form a private chain, which can be longer than any chain aware to the public. Once the public chain is within one-block distance behind, attackers reveal the longer private chain to become canonical. Hence, attackers reap the block mining awards, and public efforts are wasted. Furthermore, if attackers only withhold one block and are immediately caught up by the public, they publish their single-block private chain. In this case, even though private and public chains are of the same height, attackers can still exploit the likelihood that their private chain will eventually become

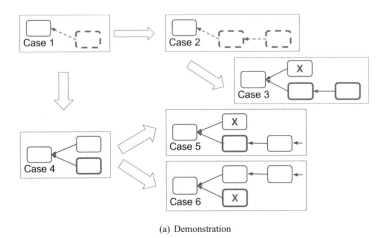

(a) Demonstration

(b) State Transition Diagram, redrawn from Figure 1 in [146].

Fig. 3.1 Demonstration and state transition diagram of selfish mining. **a** Selfish Mining can be mounted once an attacker has mined a block, e.g., the box marked in red. Instead of immediately broadcasting it, the attacker withholds it as a private chain, as illustrated by its dashed borders in Case 1. Consequently, we have Case 2 and Case 4. Case 2 denotes the possibility that the private chain continues to grow. But if the public chain catches within one block behind, the attacker broadcasts its longer private chain to become canonical and frustrate the public efforts. This is shown in Case 3, where the broadcast is illustrated by turning the private block borders from the dash to solid. Case 4 is when a public chain reaches the height of the private chain. Then the attacker also chooses to make public the private chain. The attacker reaps the benefits when his fork becomes canonical eventually, as in Case 5. He could also bear risks in Case 6 where he loses his block rewards. Despite this, in net the attacker still obtains disproportionate rewards with respect to his mining power. **b** The Markov state transition diagram for Selfish Mining, with α for the attacker's mining power and γ for the odds that the attacker's chain is accepted by the public as canonical. State 0' denotes that the attacker's chain and the public one are drawing and openly competing, amounting to the above Case 4. Hence, from this state, there are two out of three possible transitions that render attackers advantageous, as shown by two red curves shooting from State 0'. They are respectively when the attacker first mines a block on its own chain (with α probability), and when the public extends the attacker's chain (with $\gamma(1 - \alpha)$ probability). Other states labeled with integer x denote that the attacker's chain is private, and streaks ahead of the public one by x blocks. In this sense, State 2 is equivalent to the above Case 2. And its outward red curve to State 0 amounts to transition from Case 2 to Case 3, where the attacker prevails with rewards

canonical. The probability is controlled by the factor γ. Likewise, there is $1 - \gamma$ probability that the attacker's chain will not be canonical. Despite the bearing risk, researchers prove that attackers can still make a disproportionate gain. Magically, it even holds under the most unfavorable condition with $\gamma = 0$. Attackers could still achieve a super-linear payoff as long as they possess at least $\alpha = 1/3$ of the mining power. Figure 3.1 presents more details on Selfish Mining.

Selfish Mining opens up a new research direction in the mining behavior study. Not surprisingly, there come a series of tricky policies that similarly exploit the forking mechanism in Bitcoin [116, 223], as well as in Ethereum [147, 242]. In these works, researchers first hypothesize a policy, model it as a Markov chain, independently solve the equilibrium, and argue for its efficacy. For example, state transitions in Fig. 3.1a can be formally drawn as Fig. 3.1b, which is a redrawing of Fig. 1 in the original paper [146]. After taking into account their transition likelihoods, they solve the steady state probabilities and compute the net gain. The drawback of these heuristic policies is evident: there is no formal guarantee on their optimality. To fill this gap, researchers formulate the block mining game as a Markov Decision Process (MDP). Then they hinge on existing tools and frameworks to exhaust all available policies and find the optimal one. Reference [253] marks an early attempt. Researchers consider the Byzantine-controlled power and their network connectivity. The MDP formulation in [152] additionally accounts for the network delay, the staled block rate, and the ratio of eclipsed peers. Eclipsed peers are a subset of non-Byzantine peers surrounded and fouled by Byzantines. Reference [301] takes into account the varying nature of mining difficulty level. All the above analyses are from the perspective of attackers. On the other side, researchers in [155, 249] stand with non-Byzantine peers to guard against Selfish Mining. They suggest a number of indicative patterns when Selfish Mining may be under the hood. For example, an unexpected increase in staled blocks could be a potential signal. Just as shown above, a peer with less-than-majority power is incentivized to conduct the Selfish Mining. This makes it possible that more-than-one attackers are on the go. References [104, 188] explore more intricacies when there are multiple selfish miners, and they conclude Nash equilibria among them.

Selfish Mining demonstrates individual miners can benefit from the block withholding. The block withholding strategy may also find its efficacy in pooled mining as well [270]. In pooled mining, a group of individuals contribute their computation power to a shared pool. The compensation is then redistributed in proportion to their contribution shares. The pooled mining amortizes costs, reduces uncertainties, and enhances flexibility for anonymous individuals. However, anonymity also raises a vulnerability issue as follows. A pool owner may dedicate a part of its power to infiltrate competing pools, with the hope of wasting their resources. Such wastage is manifested with the intentional discarding of any discovered blocks. These blocks could generate revenues for competing pools. From the standpoint of attackers, despite their separated-out infiltration power, they lower down the mining capabilities of competitors. In net, this can translate into a revenue increase for their own pool. References [144, 202] are two independent works that delve into this interplay with finer-grained insights.

The aforementioned block withholding attack represents only one category of methods to subvert the PoW-typed blockchains, by exploiting the chain forking mechanism. Another category targets network connectivity. For example, assuming the connection profile of an honest peer is known, Byzantine peers are capable of intentionally surrounding it, effectively shielding it from the honest public. Consequently, the honest peer lives in a world completely fooled by Byzantines, unknowingly becoming an accomplice, e.g., helping to extend the Byzantine-controlled chain with the goal to surpass the public one. In a sense, the honest peer is eclipsed, hence, such an attack is known as the eclipse attack [164].

3.1.2   Proof-of-Work and Enhancements

Proof-of-work (PoW) has long been plagued by its inefficiency and excessive energy consumption. Not surprisingly, a proliferation of studies has been devoted to its enhancements. The crux of PoW is a hard-to-compute, easy-to-verify puzzle. The solution proves the resource consumption of block proposers. It demonstrates the proposers' commitment to the block validity. The intentional bar in the block proposal deters Byzantines from flooding the network. A line of work is to replace the Bitcoin puzzle with more eco-friendly ones. One notable example is Proof-of-Stake (PoS) [51]. Compared to PoW, PoS requires peers to stake cryptocurrencies before they propose blocks. Rational peers are incentivized to behave honestly, otherwise, they risk having their stakes slashed. Those with greater stakes can enjoy lower mining difficulty. Below, we compare PoS mining targeting function with that of PoW.

$$Hash(ts||...) < f(DS) \tag{3.1}$$

$$Hash(nonce||...) < f(D) \tag{3.2}$$

where f is a function that determines the required prefix zeros for block hashes. D controls the difficulty level, which unanimously applies to all peers. The staked amount of a peer determines S. Hence, S differs between peers. One may notice that any nonces that satisfy Eq. 3.2 can qualify a block in PoW. This makes it possible for proposers to test for nonces in parallel. They are capable to stack more computation resources and gain an edge in mining. In Eq. 3.1, PoS replaces the nonce with ts, a wall-clock timestamp. In other words, PoS aims to find a specific instant. With its concatenation, the resulting block hash satisfies the difficulty function. The wall clock is advancing and is fair to all block miners. Those with more resources cannot find extra edges. Instead, the difference in mining probability of peers is all attributed to S. S is dependent on peers' staked cryptocurrencies. PoW in Eq. 3.2 does not have such discriminated difficulty management. Only computation resources make the difference in PoW. This is why PoW is often criticized because of its huge power/energy consumption, while PoS is greener.

Despite the above, PoS does come with its downsides. Firstly, it suffers from the Matthew effect, that is *the rich gets richer*. Those with more cryptocurrencies can stake a greater amount, and correspondingly get more compensations. Reference [168] focuses on this the-rich-get-richer issue. Besides, PoS faces another issue on the occasion of chain forks. Block proposers are ill-incentivized to extend all forks, instead of the single longest one in PoW. It is because they get awards no matter which chains eventually win. And peers bear no additional costs to do so. This `nothing-at-stake` attack in PoS compromises the chain convergence [251]. It motivates researchers to turn around from the original resource-demanding puzzle. But this time, they aim to redirect energy consumption to useful tasks. Well-known attempts include Permacoin [211] and Filecoin [180]. Their ecosystems are centered on storage. Clients make data persistence requests, which are archived by peers. Peers repeatedly prove data availability to get awards from clients. Besides storage, some other schemes dedicate miners' resources to look for prime numbers [176], compute matrices [262], and so on. But issues are also accompanied by their offered utilities. One major concern mostly lies in the soundness and completeness of their customized puzzles. The hard-to-compute, easy-to-verify nature of most puzzles is not mathematically proved. Or, they may only be probabilistically guaranteed. The probability exists such that a non-Byzantine miner cannot pass the verification of others. Likewise, a malicious proposer may fool others with seemingly valid proof. All the above can undermine the security pillar of these distinct puzzles.

In light of this, another line of works leaves the PoW puzzle untouched, so that users can rest assured of the puzzle's robustness. They put the most effort into the PoW speedup. The most intuitive way is through re-parameterization, e.g., on the block interval. A block interval balances the performance and the security of PoW blockchains. A larger interval reduces throughput, but slashes the likelihood of peers being unsynchronized. As explained in Sect. 1.1.2, prolonged unsynchronization splits up the non-Byzantine mining power. Byzantines may find opportunities to tumble the longest chain. One may similarly reason that a smaller block size also trades the performance for the security. Despite this, some protocol designers make aggressive security assumptions. Or, they may attempt to attract investors with a more clear-to-see performance enhancement. They choose to re-parameter in the favor of performance. One may find two notable examples in Litecoin [40] and Bitcoin Cash [8]. The former reduces Bitcoin's block interval from 10 min to 2.5 min. The latter augments the block size from 1MB to 8MB.

Instead of re-parameterizing at the security expense, Bitcoin-NG [145] and Ghost [263] achieve their speedup by refining PoW. Bitcoin-NG attributes Bitcoin's low throughput to the one-time privilege of miners. In other words, a nonce only earns a miner a single chance to broadcast transactions. The intuition of Bitcoin-NG is to increase the chances per nonce. Bitcoin-NG separates blocks into key and micro blocks. A key block entails the nonce-finding process, and a micro block contains transactions. Peers compete for mining on key blocks. Bitcoin-NG allows a successful miner to continuously broadcast micro blocks until interrupted by another key block miner. Bitcoin-NG sidesteps the original performance-security trade-off. It does so by decoupling their considerations. Particularly, Bitcoin-NG establishes security by key blocks, with micro blocks for performance.

The Ghost protocol replaces the traditional longest chain rule in PoW. It sticks to the heaviest chain strategy to determine the canonical chain. Figure 3.2 shows the comparison between the Longest Chain Rule in Bitcoin and the Heaviest Chain Rule in Ethereum. Among all blocks at the same height, the one with the most descendant blocks is considered canonical. Then a canonical chain can be determined recursively. The original paper [263] extensively establishes the chain's convergence and stability. This is as opposed to the conventional PoW in Bitcoin. Bitcoin requires the contributive descendant blocks to be chained together. Evidently enough, this chaining property places more requirements on the network condition. From Sect. 1.1.2, block chaining requires network synchrony. But in Ghost, no matter which forks blocks fall in, they can all contribute to the stability of their common ancestor. From this perspective, Ghost can better tolerate the aforementioned peer inconsistencies. With the stronger tolerance on network asynchrony, the protocol adopters can safely reduce the block interval for performance considerations. For example, Ethereum chooses an aggressive 20-second interval. Despite this, it still achieves a similar security level as Bitcoin.

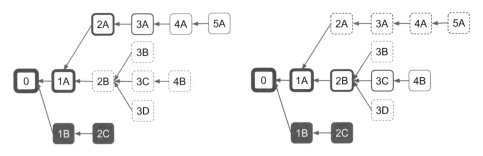

(a) Bitcoin's Longest-chain Rule   (b) Ethereum's Heaviest-chain Rule

Fig. 3.2 Comparison of the longest chain rule in Bitcoin and the heaviest chain rule in Ethereum. The longest chain, as depicted in blue, in Bitcoin is considered canonical. This is as opposed to Ethereum. Based on its Ghost protocol, for each height position, blocks with the most descendant constitute the canonical ledger. For example, Bitcoin favors Block 2A to Block 2B. It is because the former is piggybacked by a chain of three descendant blocks. But the length of the longest descendant chain behind Block 2B is two. It is the other way around under Ethereum's heaviest tree rule. All four descendant blocks are counted to back up Block 2B, and three for Block 2A. Consequently, the former is deemed canonical. From this example, the benefit of the heaviest tree rule is evident— Ethereum can make better use of uncle blocks, those not in the canonical chain such as Block 3B and 3D, to secure the canonical chain. On the other hand, the computation power contained in these uncle blocks is wasted under the longest chain rule in Bitcoin

3.1.3 Byzantine-Fault Tolerant State-Machine Replication

With blockchains, we witness the resurgence of the interest in state-machine replication (SMR) approaches for the Byzantine-fault tolerant (BFT) consensus. We have defined the consensus problem in Sect. 3.1.1. State-machine approaches are of more practical appeal to permissioned blockchains. In their operational setting, members are established, authenticated, and mutually known. Their actions are auditable. Unlike permissionless setup, protocols no longer need to carefully align incentives to peers, in a bid to economically motivate them to behave as intended. Nor do they require special treatments to deter Denial-of-Service or Sybil Attacks. This explains why security people give more weight to PoW-like consensus. In contrast, SMR is mostly applied by the Distributed Computing community. In this chapter, we examine the recent-decade progress on BFT SMR consensus. Figure 3.3 draws out their classification.

Partial Synchronous. We first restrict our attention to a class of protocols that operate under the partial synchronous network. The network model assumes the maximum propagation delay bounded but unknown. Among all, PBFT is, by no doubt, the golden standard [118]. PBFT assumes a Byzantine threshold $f < 1/3$. We assume there are a total of $N = 3F + 1$ peers, among which F are Byzantines. For example, four peers can mask at most one Byzantine. PBFT consists of two sub-protocols. One is referred to as the *Normal Flow*, which operates under gracious periods. A gracious period is when a designated peer, called `primary`, is well connected with $2F$ non-Byzantine peers. The primary prepares

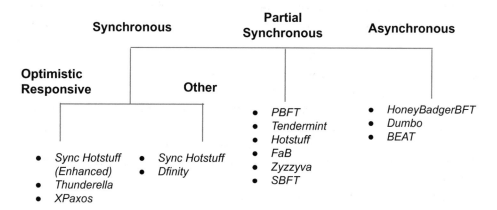

Fig. 3.3 A classification of state-machine replication approaches for Byzantine-fault tolerant consensus. Partial synchronous and synchronous protocols both employ timeouts to accommodate the maximum network delay. The wrong network assumption may damage the former's **Liveness**, and both **Safety** and **Liveness** for the latter. Synchronous protocols can further be categorized by their Optimistic Responsiveness. Optimistic responsive protocols decide proposals instantly in the Normal Flow, when the primary is non-Byzantine and well-connected to other peers. They use timeouts during the View Change. Born without timeouts, asynchronous protocols employ randomness

a predicate-conforming proposal, e.g., a block with valid transactions in the blockchain context. The proposal is broadcasted to all other peers (Pre-prepare Phase). Each recipient independently verifies the proposal and checks it did not ever cast a vote for other proposals. (A vote is unique for each consensus instance.) If so, the recipient broadcasts a digitally signed message to indicate a YES vote (Prepare Phase). The signature is vital for the message authenticity. Those receiving self-inclusive, $2F + 1$ consistent YES votes are eligible to make another full broadcast with Commit messages (Commit Phase). In the end, a proposal supported by self-inclusive, $2F + 1$ Commit messages can be safely decided by recipients. Here, one may notice that the $2F + 1$ quorum is a must to defy the primary's misconduct. For example, consider the scenario when the Byzantine primary equivocates. That is, it sends different proposals to disjoint sets of peers, as an attempt to foul them with divergent proposals and to break the aforementioned **Safety** property. However, this is impossible as a decided proposal must be YES-voted by at least $2F + 1$ peers. A simple contradiction can prove it. The first Prepare broadcast is to accumulate such support. Remember that there are at most F Byzantines within a total of $3F + 1$ processes. Two decided proposals indicate there must be at least $F + 1$ peers that voted for both. (The intersection is computed as $(2F + 1) + (2F + 1) - (3F + 1) = F + 1$.) In turn, this implies a duplicated vote from a non-Byzantine, protocol-abiding one, given there are only F Byzantines. Clearly, this breaks the assumption of non-Byzantine peer behavior at the Prepare phase (unique YES-votes). Though **Safety** remains intact, the primary can still pretend to be non-responsive. Then **Liveness** is in danger as the execution can be delayed permanently. The second sub-protocol, the *View Change*, is to complement the Normal Flow for this issue. Basically, peers monitor the consensus progress, which is dependent on the primary. If they find it is stuck, they may jointly attempt to replace the primary. This is in hope of a new non-Byzantine primary to carry on the execution. One key challenge is to preserve the previously decided proposals across views for **Safety**. The additional precaution necessitates a Commit phase in the second broadcast. (The proof of how Commit broadcast upholds View Change is non-trivial. One may find more details in the original paper [118].) **Validity** trivially holds. There are two popular PBFT protocol implementations, BFT-SMART and IBFT. BFT-SMART puts modularity at the forefront of its design so as to facilitate customizations [107]. On the other hand, IBFT is specially tailored for the ledger abstraction of blockchains [218]. It is already in production use in Quorum. IBFT additionally accommodates the dynamic change of consensus groups.

Despite its popularity, PBFT is flawed by its limited scalability. This is easy to see from the two phases of the all-to-all broadcast, as shown in Fig. 3.4a, which incur quadratic message complexity. Tendermint[1] reduces the complexity to linear with aggregate signatures [111]. Aggregate signatures enable a primary to combine multiple peer-signed votes into a single message. As shown in Fig. 3.4b, the linear message complexity comes from the fact that the primary acts as a relay to distribute the message and convey the votes, instead of an all-to-all

---

[1] Here, we consider the permissioned version of Tendermint, where peers are determined. The permissionless counterpart employs Proof-of-Stake to elect peers and then carries the voting protocol [169].

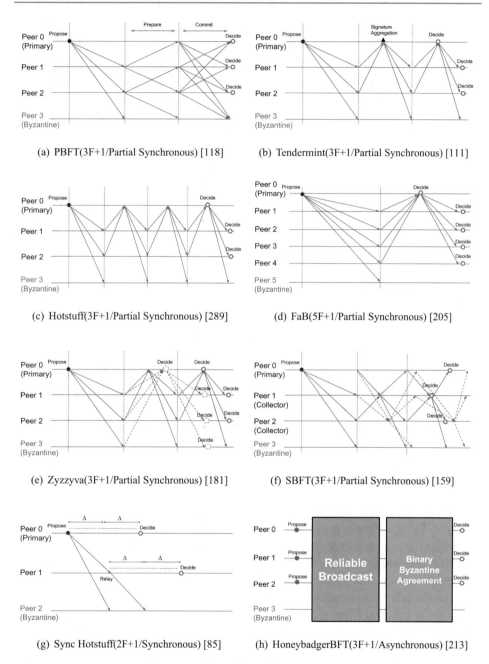

(a) PBFT(3F+1/Partial Synchronous) [118]

(b) Tendermint(3F+1/Partial Synchronous) [111]

(c) Hotstuff(3F+1/Partial Synchronous) [289]

(d) FaB(5F+1/Partial Synchronous) [205]

(e) Zyzzyva(3F+1/Partial Synchronous) [181]

(f) SBFT(3F+1/Partial Synchronous) [159]

(g) Sync Hotstuff(2F+1/Synchronous) [85]

(h) HoneybadgerBFT(3F+1/Asynchronous) [213]

Fig. 3.4 Message patterns of state-machine replication approaches for Byzantine-fault tolerant consensus (normal flow), with their fault tolerance level and the assumed network model. Notation xF+1 indicates the tolerance level, e.g., 3F+1 implies a totality of four peers can mask a single Byzantine broadcast. The message linearity makes Tendermint comparable to PoW. Hence, it becomes extremely attractive under a global P2P network, where a large number of peers communicate in a bandwidth-limited network. Despite this, the message linearity deprives Tendermint of View Change **Responsiveness**. Particularly, during View Changes, PBFT peers can take immediate action once receiving enough messages. On the other hand, Tendermint needs to additionally wait for a period of time. The waiting duration must be greater than the maximum network delay. Otherwise, **Liveness** can be flawed, i.e., peers remain in an undecided state infinitely. HotStuff managed to combine both message linearity and responsiveness [289], but it bears an additional message round as seen in Fig. 3.4c.

Another line of partial synchronous BFT SMR is on the balance between message trips and fault tolerance levels. Excluding the initial proposal broadcast, PBFT, Tendermint, and HotStuff respectively take 2, 2, and 3 message rounds. Fast Byzantine (FaB), shown in Fig. 3.4d, further decreases the number of rounds to 1 at the cost of $f < 1/5$ [205]. In other words, FaB needs 6 peers to tolerate a single Byzantine. Correspondingly, a primary needs to contact $4F$ other peers out of a total of $5F + 1$. Despite being conditioned by the single-shot, FaB proves it matches the lower bound on the tolerance level. Zyzzyva demonstrates that message trips and fault tolerance can be adjusted dynamically in the same run [181]. The enabler is its speculative execution, as Fig. 3.4e illustrates. Concretely, Zyzzyva starts with a conservative assumption, i.e., $f < 1/3$. If the primary is fortunate to contact more-than-expected non-Byzantine peers, then the fast path can be triggered. Like FaB, Zyzzyva's fast path achieves the consensus in a single round. If not attaining the required connectivity, Zyzzyva would fall back to the conventional two-phase slow path. But an additional fast path option inevitably adds more complexity to the protocol reasoning, which is already hard enough. Specifically, now there are four possible scenarios for view changes; each of two consecutive views can be either in the fast path or the slow path. For the protocol security, **Safety** and **Liveness** must both hold in each scenario. Empirical evidence shows that such a guarantee is far trickier to achieve than expected [83]. SBFT can be seen as a scalability-oriented PBFT variant that absorbs many engineering practices [159]. Besides the linear message complexity from Tendermint and the speculative fast path from Zyzzyva, SBFT separates the duties of primary peers. This is shown in Fig. 3.4f. Apart from the proposal broadcast, primaries offload the vote collection job to C-collectors, a subset of other peers. Each C-collector assumes an identical role, i.e., aggregating signatures and relaying votes. Redundant C-collectors improve resilience, as a single collector can carry on the execution and other stragglers just serve as backup. It increases the likelihood that a well-connected C-collector contacts enough peers to trigger the fast path. All the aforementioned protocols use timeouts. The timeout duration accommodates the worst-case network connectivity. Timeout peers may assume the primary failure and initiate the view change for the progress. This shows why the network synchrony is vital for the protocol's **Liveness**. But on the flip side, **Safety** is always guaranteed by the set intersection rule as illustrated in the PBFT case. Their always-safe nature explains why these protocols especially accommodate a partial synchronous network, where the delay is not known but bounded. Practically, protocol implementations can safely test for different timeouts based on the progress feedback. Usually, protocol implementations adopt an exponential back-off mechanism to adjust the timeouts.

As we have seen, all the aforementioned partial synchronous protocols call for a primary to drive the protocol running. But these protocols differ in their designs and whether this primary shall remain fixed. In particular, PBFT, SBFT, FaB, and Zyzzyva stick to the stable leaders—a designated primary can carry on more-than-one consensus instance, unless it is out of reach or is found to exhibit Byzantine behaviors. In contrast, HotStuff and Tendermint rotate primaries per instance, amounting to performing view changes in each round. The benefit of rotating primaries is fairness: it prevents the designated primary from selectively filtering proposals. But the primary-rotating mechanism requires efficient view changes. The view changes of HotStuff and Tendermint are only of linear complexity in terms of the number of peers, while in other protocols these are quadratic.

Synchronous. Now we turn back to another class of protocols, which operate under a more restrictive network model. These protocols need to be aware of δ, the maximum network propagation delay. The communication delay of two non-Byzantine peers is always bounded by δ, despite Byzantines' manipulation. The timeliness assumption enables protocols to rely on δ for the **Safety**. As we can see later, this offers tremendous convenience. For example, consider a simple protocol as follows. There is a designated primary to broadcast proposals. When peers receive a valid proposal, they re-broadcast it and promise not to respond to other valid proposals. After waiting for 2δ without receiving other conflicting ones, a peer can safely decide. The safety reasoning is straightforward: suppose the peer relays the proposal at time t, then all non-Byzantine peers will receive by time $t + \delta$. If no conflicts are received after $t + 2\delta$, no other peers could relay any conflicted proposals at $t + \delta$. This implies that the relayed proposal is ubiquitously accepted. Sync HotStuff [85], drawn in Fig. 3.4g, and Dfinity [84] follow this paradigm with their slight customizations. Due to the synchronous assumption, their fault tolerance is enhanced to $f < 1/2$. Intuitively, this is the upper bound to ensure Byzantines are the minority. But their drawback is evident, as they forgo **Responsiveness**. In a nutshell, there is an explicit δ-measured waiting period in the critical path of execution. XPaxos [195], Thunderella [230], and an enhanced version of Sync HotStuff [85] move this delay out of the Normal Flow to the View Change. In a sense, during gracious execution, protocol executions are entirely message-driven. But on the occasion that a Byzantine primary triggers a View Change, there is a timer on each peer. During view changes, peers need to explicitly wait for the timer expiration before taking any actions. In synchronous protocols, the waiting duration requires special care. If it is below the actual propagation delay, previously decided proposals may be subject to loss in the new view. It thereby compromises **Safety**. This is opposed to the above partial synchronous protocols, where timeout durations only affect **Liveness**. Considering their Responsiveness under their Normal Flow, we classify this subset of synchronous protocols into the Optimistic Responsive sub-category. Flexible BFT aims for a one-size-fits-all design, such that clients with different network assumptions can coexist [204]. Assumptions can be on the network synchrony nature, propagation bound, etc. Clients may apply their own assumption-specific rules to decide on proposals. Those with correct assumptions are guaranteed to reach a common decision.

Asynchronous. Timeouts are extensively employed in all the above protocols. However, in a realistic deployment, timeouts are finicky to tune. Synchronous protocols must take a conservative network assumption for **Safety**. But a large timeout negatively affects their progress. A short timeout makes partial synchronous protocols vulnerable to network perturbation. This can be evidenced by frequent view changes, which in turn drive consensus to a halt. Then one may naturally ask: can we devise a timeout-free consensus protocol that achieves both **Safety** and **Liveness** (as well as **Validity**) in an asynchronous network? Unfortunately, the FLP Theorem rules out this possibility for any deterministic protocols [148]. For any deterministic protocol, this implies that there always exists a forever-running consensus round (the peers may remain in an undecided state infinitely). In spite of the FLP-based setback, there is another direction for timeout-free consensus: the stochasticity. There are approaches that employ randomness to diminish the non-termination likelihood to arbitrarily small. HoneyBadgerBFT exemplifies this line of efforts [213]. The protocol advances in asynchronous rounds, which do not involve timers. As shown in Fig. 3.4h, there are two phases in a round. In the first phase, each of the N peers initiates the Reliable Broadcast (RBC) sub-protocol [109] to reliably disseminate their proposal to all other peers. In the second phase, peers concurrently run N instances of Asynchronous Binary Agreement [219], where the decision value is restricted to either 0 or 1. The i-th decision indicates whether the i-th proposal shall be included. In HoneyBadgerBFT, its second binary consensus phase manifests the randomness. It terminates at time t with probability $O(1 - 2^{-t})$, which converges to 0 as t approaches infinity. As the carry-on work of HoneyBadgerBFT, Dumbo combines the two phases more judiciously, in an attempt to reduce the number of messages [160]. Both works stand for a single design point that favors throughput over latency. In contrast, BEAT adds flexibility and versatility at the forefront [140]. It proposes a suite of asynchronous protocols that come with different flavors on latency, throughput, bandwidth, and scalability. As such, clients may explore more meaningful trade-offs. In all, the timeout-free design enables asynchronous protocols to closely track the network conditions. Besides, by comparing them with other message patterns in Fig. 3.4, one may observe asynchronous protocols elevate the level of decentralization. There is no privileged primary peer that drives the consensus. Though primaries in other protocols are subject to inspections, there are possibilities that they may selectively filter out certain proposals. Or, they may bias their proposal orders in their favor. By treating peers equally, asynchronous protocols eliminate such exploitations, thus being more robust to censorship.

We draw the message patterns of some of the aforementioned protocols in Fig. 3.4 and tabulate their statistical properties in Table 3.1. Message patterns reflect their Normal Flow behavior. Protocols run the Normal Flow during the gracious period when primaries are non-Byzantine and well-connected to other non-Byzantine peers.

Table 3.1 Properties of Byzantine-fault tolerant state-machine replications. N denotes the number of peers to mask a single failure. Delay measures the message round from a primary proposing a request until at least a peer commits it. Delay is only appliable to protocols for the partial synchronous network

Protocol	Message complexity		Normal flow delay	View change responsiveness
	Normal flow	View change		
PBFT	$O(N^2)$	$O(N^2)$	3	✓
Tendermint	$O(N)$	$O(N)$	3	✗
HotStuff	$O(N)$	$O(N)$	4	✓
FaB	$O(N)$	$O(N^2)$	2	✓
Zyzzyva	$O(N)$	$O(N^2)$	2 (Fast Path)/4 (Slow Path)	✓
SBFT	$O(N)$	$O(N^2)$	2 (Fast Path)/4 (Slow Path)	✓
Sync HotStuff	$O(N)$	$O(N)$	N.A.	✓
HoneyBadgerBFT	$O(N)$		N.A.	N.A.

- Figure 3.4a: PBFT incurs a quadratic message complexity due to all-to-all broadcasts.
- Figure 3.4b: Tendermint reduces the complexity to linear with primaries aggregating signatures and relay messages.
- Figure 3.4c: HotStuff adds an additional message round for the View Change responsiveness, while retaining linearity.
- Figure 3.4d: FaB achieves the single-shot consensus at the expense of fault tolerance.
- Figure 3.4e: Zyzzyva optimistically attempts the one-shot consensus (dashed lines), and falls back to the conventional two-phase approach (solid lines) if the attempt fails.
- Figure 3.4f: SBFT offloads signature aggregations from a single primary to multiple collector peers. It provides redundancy to avoid stragglers.
- Figure 3.4g: Sync HotStuff peers wait for δ in the critical path on deciding proposals.
- Figure 3.4h: HoneyBadgerBFT employs Reliable Broadcast (First Phase) and Asynchronous Binary Agreement (Second Phase) in tandem to achieve probabilistic consensus.

3.2 Concurrency

In Sect. 2.3, we discuss concurrency in blockchains and distributed databases. As we have seen earlier, databases put much weight on concurrency for speedup. Blockchains execute transactions serially based on the ledger order. Concretely, the consensus orders transactions in the form of a ledger. Based on transaction-encoded contexts, peers independently invoke contracts to initiate state transitions. We refer to this execution paradigm as **Order-execute** (OX). Even though the sequentiality shall make blockchain more predictable, smart contract behaviors are far trickier than expected. This is evidenced by a number of buggy contracts in Ethereum. Exploitative transactions targeting their vulnerabilities have led to substantial financial losses. Worse still, owing to Ethereum's permissionless nature, attackers can easily escape the consequences of their actions. In this chapter, we will go deeper into these vulnerabilities, attacks, and mitigations.

The above-mentioned attacks are partly attributed to Ethereum's transaction structure. Transactions only carry contract-invoking contexts. Clients may not fully anticipate their effects when transactions are executed. To reduce uncertainties, Hyperledger Fabric introduces the **Execute-order-validate** (EOV) execution paradigm [91]. This paradigm allows clients to get the first peek of transaction effects before sending them to the consensus. EOV paradigm also comes with one prominent downside: in-ledger transactions may be aborted in order to abide by the ledger-imposed sequentiality constraints. Later, we will use a concrete example to demonstrate this downside, so as to motivate the necessity of subsequent techniques for its mitigation.

At the end of this chapter, we systematically compare the two execution paradigms and review novel execution paradigms beyond them.

3.2.1 Order-Execute Paradigm and Security Implications

As an order-execute, permissionless blockchain, Ethereum draws attacks at an unprecedented scale. Let's first refresh on its contract management lifecycle, and then we will explain what may go wrong. A contract developer codifies a contract in Solidity, a high-level language. The developer locally compiles the contract into bytecode and broadcasts it with a Deployment transaction. By consensus, the Deployment transaction disseminates the code to each peer. Upon contract deployment, peers also reach an agreement on the contract identifier and its initial state. The Ethereum protocol mandates peers to organize states in MPT for ease of synchronization. Contract states are subject to change by subsequent Invocation transactions. These transactions carry contract invocation contexts. Contexts may include a callee contract identifier, parameters, and a caller signature, among others. Likewise, they are pre-compiled into binary forms before broadcasting. Each peer independently runs binary-coded transactions on Ethereum Virtual Machine (EVM). EVM deterministically transforms the execution into MPT modifications. EVM's runtime semantics are also a part of the protocol, such that protocol-abiding peers shall reach identical states.

Just like coding in any high-level language, programming defects are inevitable. Contracts may also behave in unintended ways under corner cases. But their effects are far more detrimental, as contracts are usually financially involved. Besides, once a contract is deployed, its logic is public to everyone. Without careful access control, any anony-

```
13   address admin;
14
15        // A would-be constructor is misspelled and it could be purposely invoked by
              any clients.
16        ContracTA() { admin = msg.sender; }
17        ...
18   }
```

Listing 3.1 A Misspelled Constructor (Language-level Vulnerability)

```
1    // In Victim contract, the withdraw function forgets to zero out the recipient
           balance before calling the external contract for the transfer. It leaves an
           opportunity for the Attacker contract to reenter into the Victim's method
           for the repeated withdrawal.
2
3    contract Victim {
4        mapping (address => uint) private bal_;
5        function withdraw(address recipient) public {
6            uint amount = bal_[recipient];
7            if amount > 0 recipient.transfer(amount);
8            bal_[recipient] = 0;
9        }
10   }
11
12   contract Attacker {
13       uint my_bal_;
14       function transfer(uint amount) public {
15           my_bal_ += amount;
16           Victim.withdraw(self); // reentrancy point
17       }
18   }
```

Listing 3.2 A Reentrancy Vulnerability Owing to an External Call (Runtime-level Vulnerability)

mous attacker could easily exploit the contract's flaws. Worse still, the blockchain-provided immutability prohibits any patching or fixing. We generally classify contract vulnerabilities into the following three categories. Our classification methodology is partly inspired by [95]. First, the language-level vulnerability comes from the misuse of high-level language features. Second, the runtime-level vulnerability is due to the miscalculation of the EVM runtime behavior. Third, the platform-level vulnerability is peculiar to the blockchain forking mechanism. Below, we give an example of a flawed contract in each category.

Language-level. Solidity regards a function with an identical name as its contract as a constructor. A constructor is for one-time execution upon the contract deployment. It is usually dedicated to critical state initializations. However, some careless programmers may misspell it, as shown in Listing 3.1. Then, the Solidity compiler treats it as a regular function, which is unintentionally open for access to any invoker. Likewise, Solidity assumes a function without the explicit access declaration for public use. It may also expose visibility erroneously. Fledgling programmers tend to ignore Solidity exceptions. Their mishandling proves to be hazardous as well [200]. The above seemingly intuitive programming mistakes

```
1   contract Item {
2       uint quantity_;
3       uint price_;
4       // Block proposers are capable to bias the order between a transaction
            invoking set_price() and the one invoking buy() in their proposed block
            , so as to maximize their interest.
5
6       function set_price(uint price) only admin {
7           price_ = price;
8       }
9       function buy(uint payments) {
10          uint buy_quantity = payments / price_;
11          quantity_ -= buy_quantity;
12          msg.sender.transfer(buy_quantity);
13      }
14  }
```

Listing 3.3 A Transaction-ordering Dependency in a Contract

are not without occurrence. These can be seen in many real-world contracts and attacks [55, 238].

Runtime-level. The EVM runtime behavior gets especially convoluted when a contract calls another one. Worse still, that callee contract can be external and under the manipulation of attackers. This is particularly dangerous as the caller contract cannot anticipate the callee's behavior. Despite this, the caller contract blindly gives up the execution flow. Consider the Victim contract which allows an invoker to specify a recipient address. Listing 3.2 demonstrates an example. The address is from the recipient of the cryptocurrency withdrawal, which is achieved by calling its transfer function. However, an attacker can intentionally craft the transfer as follows. Besides crediting the received amount, transfer invokes Victim's Withdraw again in a nested manner. In the re-entrant call, the Victim still finds the recipient's non-zero balance. Then it continues to perform the withdrawal over and over again. Interestingly enough, such recursion allows Attacker to easily drain the Victim's balance. One fundamental reason is that the Victim contract zeros out the recipient balance at the very end. It leaves an invalid, halfway state for the external call, which is out of its control. Then the contract developer cannot fully grasp the EVM runtime behavior, making exploitative room for attackers. This Reentrancy Vulnerability is the culprit of the infamous DAO Hack [252]. The DAO Hack teaches a million-dollar lesson on contract security. Some other unusual EVM semantics could also be dangerous. They include but are not limited to integer overflow and call-stack depth limit [17].

Platform-level. Contracts with platform-level vulnerabilities are usually owing to their developers' ignorance of blockchain mechanisms. Particularly, they neglect the fact that block proposers can selectively pick transactions and their orders. However, transactions may have stakes in their order. Consider the contract in Listing 3.3. A specific owner can invoke set_price for an item. And any invoker (message sender) can call buy to purchase them at the stated price. Evidently, the order matters when two transactions invoke set_price and buy. Aware of a buy transaction, a block proposer could maliciously put ahead a `set_price` one. It deliberately increases the item price, far greater than the amount when a client invokes `buy` transaction. When the `buy` transaction takes effect, the client suffers from an unexpected price surge. Beyond the transaction-order dependency [200], contracts contingent on timestamps and block hashes are all susceptible to the above manipulations. Block hashes are often used for randomness sources when contracts involve a stochastic process [50].

Another platform-level vulnerability is termed Verifier's Dilemma [203]. Unlike the above, it poses a security threat to the entire system rather than only to contract developers. Verifier's Dilemma is rooted in the blockchain incentive mechanism. The successful block proposer solely reaps all the transaction fees. Other verifiers are obliged to re-run the transactions on EVM to check their validity. But the verification is without compensation. Think about the scenario when verifiers face transactions with remarkable validation overhead. Those verifiers are ill-incentivized to skip it and naively assume their validity. By doing so, they could gain an edge on the next block mining. Given this negligence, malicious proposers are emboldened to include ill-executed transactions. These transactions may deviate from EVM semantics. Or they can deliberately include a heavy-weighted transaction to discourage others' verification. (It does no economic harm to proposers in terms of transaction fees, as proposers are both payers and beneficiaries for the transaction.) With Verifier's Dilemma, illegal transactions may find likelihoods to bypass the consensus and become persisted.

Prevention and Mitigation. Considering their tremendous popularity and vulnerable nature, a growing number of programming guidelines and tools are proposed to contract developments. Reference [257] provides a novel viewpoint on contract anomaly, by drawing an analogy with concurrency bugs in distributed computing. More practically, contract programmers may refer to [32] for a summary of best practices. Or, they may turn to professional companies for code audits [67]. We have also seen a number of contract analysis tools, such as Oyente [200], Maian [226], Teether [182], and Discover [21]. Targeting Solidity, they construct a program control graph and perform symbolic execution. These analysis tools help to proactively understand a contract behavior. In the meantime, there is steady progress on the Solidity refinement. For example, from the proposal in [15], developers can explicitly mark a constructor function, instead of implicit naming. Beyond Solidity, new EVM-compatible languages are appearing. Some high-level languages like Vyper [74] simplify Solidity, by removing its problematic features. Codes in intermediate-level languages like Scilla [258] can also compile into EVM-compatible binaries. Intermediate-level languages are more amenable to the formal analysis on their correctness. At last, oracles are effective to eliminate bugs born from the proposer-introduced bias. Oracles are data feeds that connect blockchains with the outside world [31]. Their services are extensively equipped for fairness and integrity guarantee [2, 110]. The imported randomness from oracles can be more trustworthy, compared to the conventional approach powered by block hashes. Verifier's Dilemma can be cured by imposing a maximum gas limit on an Ethereum block. The

cap restricts the overall complexity of internal transactions and moderates the verification
overhead for verifiers.

3.2.2 Execute-Order-Validate Paradigm and Transaction Aborts

Hyperledger Fabric proposes the execute-order-validate (EOV) paradigm. It partly addresses
the security issues of order-execute (OX) blockchains, such as Ethereum. The EOV paradigm
introduces an Execution (or Simulation) phase at the start of the transaction lifecycle. In this
phase, clients tentatively seek simulation results for their requests. Aware of their effects,
they may then decide whether to generate transactions from the results and submit them.
As opposed to OX transactions which contain pre-execution contexts, EOV transactions
reduce uncertainties by directly carrying post-execution effects. But certainties come with
the cost of a concurrency mechanism and aborted transactions. These are necessary to make
overall transactions effects abide by the ledger order [91]. In other words, peer databases
will reflect a state as if executing these transactions in the ledger-specified order. We refer to
this order-abiding property as Serializability. Figure 3.5 together with Table 3.2 illustrates
the above with an example on Hyperledger Fabric. The example is adapted from [248].

Fabric assigns three roles to computing nodes, even though they are mutually distrusted.
These roles are (i) *client* who proposes a transaction, (ii) *peer* who *executes* the proposals
from clients, and (iii) *orderer* which *orders* transactions, arranges them into blocks and
strings blocks into a ledger. Orderers collectively run a consensus protocol in order to settle
the transaction order.

The blockchain state after applying block transactions is organized as a collection of
versioned key-value entries. An entry consists of (`key`, `ver`, `val`), where `key` uniquely
identifies the entry, and `ver` and `val` are its latest version and value, respectively. Fur-

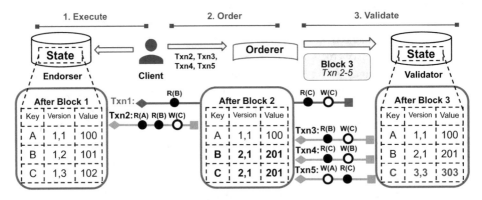

Fig. 3.5 An example of transactions workflow in execute-order-validate blockchains. An arrow
denotes the execution (simulation) phase of a transaction, e.g., Txn1 starts its execution after block
1 and finishes after block 2

Table 3.2 A summary of the transactions in Fig. 3.5. Staled reads and installed writes are colored in red and blue, respectively. The symbols ✓, ✗, and **N.A.** respectively denote committed, aborted, or not-allowed transactions. This table is based on [248]

		Txn1		Txn2		Txn3	Txn4	Txn5
Readset	Key	B	C	A	B	B	C	C
	Version	1,2	2,1	1,1	1,2	2,1	2,1	2,1
Writeset	Key	C		C		C	B	A
	Value	301		302		**303**	304	305
Commit status		**N.A.**		✗		✓	✗	✗

thermore, ver represents a two-value tuple reflecting the sequence in the ledger of the transaction that updates the entry. Taking the example in Fig. 3.5, the entry (C, (2, 1), 201) in the state after applying block 2 denotes that the latest value for the key C is 201. This value is lastly installed by the first transaction of block 2. With the above notations in mind, we go on to elaborate on the three phases in the workflow of a transaction.

Execute. In this phase, clients propose transactions to a subset of endorsing peers (this is a configurable subset of peers). Proposals include contexts to invoke smart contracts. Each endorsing peer invokes contracts speculatively. The peer returns the simulated execution results endorsed by its signature. The results consist of two value sets, namely the *readset* and the *writeset*. The former includes keys and versions of the read entries. The latter includes the simulation-computed state updates. Table 3.2 summarizes the two sets for all the transactions in Fig. 3.5. During a transaction's execution (simulation), Fabric keeps a read lock on the entire state database. This implies that transactions reading across blocks, such as Txn1 in Fig. 3.5, are impossible. The client must collect a number of identical simulation results as stated in the endorsement policy, so that they can package them into a single qualified transaction. The client can then submit the fully fledged transaction to orderers. Then, the transaction's lifecycle enters the second phase.

Order. In this phase, orderers receive transactions from clients. Orderers are responsible to settle a total order of the transactions. This is illustrated in Fig. 3.5. To determine the order, orderers collectively run a consensus protocol. Each orderer employs the same criteria to batch transactions into blocks based on the agreed-upon transaction order after running the consensus. The criteria could be a cap on the block size. In Fig. 3.5, for instance, Txn2, Txn3, Txn4, and Txn5 reach the orderers. Orderers run the consensus to agree upon their order. Based on this consistent order and batching criteria, each orderer shall reach the same sequence of blocks, i.e., block 3 with Txn2 to Txn5. Here, we assume a block contains at most four transactions.

Validate. This phase kicks in on peers after they receive a block from the orderers. Peers sequentially validate transactions considering the corresponding endorsement policy and the transaction serializability. Peers inspect the endorsement policy by examining endorsers' signatures attached in the transactions. Peers determine a transaction's serializability by checking the staleness of its readset. A transaction is considered invalid (unserializable) if it reads an outdated entry. The outdated entry is owing to another transaction committed after the execution phase of the invalid transaction. For example, in Fig. 3.5, transaction Txn2 in block 3 is unserializable because it reads the key B with version (1, 2) from block 1. However, this version is outdated during the validation phase of Txn2, as the latest version in block 2 is already (2, 1). Unlike Txn2, Txn3 satisfies the serializability. Hence Fabric, during the validation of block 3, refreshes the version of key C version to (3, 3). Txn3 invalidates transactions Txn4 and Txn5, because both transactions read an outdated version of key C from block 2. Consequently, only transaction Txn3 is included (committed) in block 3 after the validation phase. Other aborted transactions (e.g., Txn2, Txn4, and Txn5) do not have the opportunity to persist their effects to the blockchain state.

Reducing Aborts. In EOV blockchains, transactions with staled reads are undesirable since they waste the system throughput. Unlike databases, blockchains' processing capacity is inherently limited by factors other than data processing [260]. These factors may include consensus, cryptographic operations, and others.

Can we reorganize the transactions in the ledger, in a way that minimizes these aborts while retaining Serializability? On this challenge, Fabric++ marks an early attempt [260]. Researchers identify similarities between the optimistic concurrency control (OCC) in databases and the EOV pipeline. After grounding blockchain transactions into the context of databases, researchers conclude that read-write dependencies between transactions are causes of aborts. For example, in Fig. 3.5, Txn4 is dependent on Txn3. It is because the latter updates key C, rendering the Txn4's read stale. Given this, Fabric++ introduces a reordering step in orderers, just before they form a block. This step constructs a transaction graph with respect to read-write dependencies. Figure 3.6 shows the graph corresponding to the example in Fig. 3.5. Fabric++ then looks for problematic transactions that contribute to the most dependency cycles, such as Txn4 in this case. After removing them, the rest are sequenced according to their topological order. For the example in Fig. 3.5, an order could be Txn5, Txn3, and Txn2 for block 3. Transaction reordering in Fabric++ eliminates read-write dependencies in the same block, but not across blocks. Though Txn2 is dependency-free in block 3, it cannot pass the above Serializability checking. It is due to the staled version of its read key B, due to a transaction in the previous block 2. Despite this, Fabric++ can still save one more transaction compared to the original Fabric.

FabricSharp goes deeper in this direction [248]. In FabricSharp, researchers make a key observation on another cause of excessive aborts, that is, the Serializability restriction. If the transaction effect is relaxed to conform to **any** serial order (not necessarily to the unique ledger order), more transactions could be recovered. By gauging Serializability, Fabric-Sharp demonstrates a more fine-grained concurrency control approach, to the point where false aborts are completely ruled out. It is because FabricSharp considers more transaction dependencies besides the read-write ones. In addition, FabricSharp can resolve dependencies across blocks. This is opposed to Fabric++, where unserializable to-abort transactions,

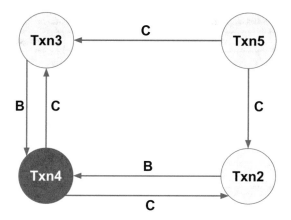

Fig. 3.6 A transaction graph for Fabric++ for the example in Fig. 3.5. An arrow labeled with A implies that a head and a tail transaction respectively reads and writes the key A. The head transaction can avoid its abort by being placed ahead of the tail transaction. Fabric++ removes transactions that contribute to most cycles, and sequences the rest to align with the dependency orders. For the example in Fig. 3.5, the removed transaction is Txn4, and the order for the rest could be Txn5, Txn3, and Txn2

such as Txn2 in the above example, could still exist in the ledger. FabricSharp additionally analyzes the security implications of transaction reordering under blockchains' hostile operating environment. In the end, HyperLedgerLab produces a fair testbed to evaluate the concurrency behavior of the above Fabric variants [119].

3.2.3 OX Versus EOV, and Others

We systemize the comparison between the two execution paradigms, as shown in Table 3.3. We organize our systemization using the below properties.

Predictiveness. As mentioned, EOV blockchain behavior incurs fewer uncertainties, as transactions carry the post-execution effects. This is in contrast with the OX blockchains with pre-invocation contexts in their transactions.

Parallelism. The EOV paradigm favors parallelism. This is because transactions can be concurrently simulated. The key parallelism enabler is the read-only nature in their first execution phase. Peers simulate contract invocation for their effects. They do not persist in these effects until the validation phase. OX processes transactions literally in a serial manner based on the ledger order.

Confidentiality. EOV restricts contract invocations to specific peers. Moreover, transactions only expose their effects, not the entire context. In OX, contract logic and invocation contexts are all publicly available on the ledger.

Table 3.3 Comparisons between Execute-order-validate and Execute-order Paradigms

	Execute-order-validate	Order-execute
Predictiveness	✓	
Parallelism	✓	
Confidentiality	✓	
Modularity	✓	
Abort-free		✓
Anonymity		✓
State Integrity		✓

Modularity. EOV separates blockchain nodes into distinct roles. A transaction's lifecycle is broken down into three phases. Compared to the monolithic architecture of OX, modularity brings flexibility. For example, in Fabric, an endorsement policy specifies the trust level of contract invocations. The specification is manifested as the minimum number of endorsing peers to support an invocation result. In OX, this threshold for a qualified transaction is bound by the consensus protocol, not being at the discretion of contract deployers. For example, Ethereum with the PoW consensus requires the majority of peers to agree on transaction effects.

Abort-free. As discussed for EOV, transaction aborts are inevitable under the Serializability constraints. Fundamentally, it is because EOV separates transaction execution and state persistence phases. OX does not do the separation and hence there is no transaction abort.

Anonymity. Upon the receipt of a block, OX blockchains re-execute transactions to verify their validity. Instead, Endorsers' signatures prove the EOV transaction validity. Evidently enough, the signature-attested scheme requires authenticated peers. Hence, the EOV paradigm is not compatible with the anonymous property of permissionless blockchains.

State Integrity. Another drawback of EOV phase separation is that peers can no longer verify the integrity of the post-execution state during the consensus. It is because EOV performs the consensus before applying the transactions' effects. Hence, Hyperledger Fabric does not come with a Merkle tree, which is used in Ethereum, to protect state integrity. Instead, it relies on the permissioned assumption for query integrity, i.e., peers must attach their signatures in responses as proof.

Other Paradigms. At last, we review some novel execution paradigms beyond EOV and OX. These proposals aim to join both paradigms to achieve the best of both worlds. ParBlockchain introduces OXII, which adds parallelism on top of OX [89]. OXII establishes transaction dependency during the ordering phase. The dependency information is exposed to peers, so that they can execute transactions in parallel on the best-effort basis. Reference [134] shares a similar spirit, with an attempt to introduce parallelism on OX. References [89, 134] differ at their implementation level. The former harnesses parallelism between processes on a single peer, while the latter focuses on parallelism among peers. XOX improves on the EOV paradigm, focusing on reducing transactions aborts [156]. But unlike Fabric++ and FabricSharp, XOX brings architectural improvements. Particularly, XOX proposes a re-execution phase after ordering. The re-execution phase attempts to recover would-be aborted transactions. XOX achieves this by running a patch-up code. The patch-up run refreshes transactions with staled reads with the latest values. A similar re-architecture on EOV can be found in [266]. While the original Fabric processes blocks in lock steps, [266] pipelines this procedure. A block's transaction validation can be concurrent to previous blocks' state persistence. The pipeline makes better use of computation resources, and it preserves the security and Serializability.

3.3 Storage

In Sect. 2.4, we show that blockchain storage is centered on a ledger. The sequential ledger encodes a full transaction history. This is opposed to databases which only maintain the latest states. Blockchain states are derived from its ledger. For example, the collection of unspent transaction outputs constitutes the state in Bitcoin. Script-protected cryptocurrencies keep the available balances that their owners (holders of associated private keys) can manipulate. Some contract-enabled blockchains explicitly maintain states in an authenticated data structure, such as Merkle Patricia Trie. This is to protect state integrity and facilitate query proof.

In this chapter, we zoom in on the latest studies on blockchain storage. The first is the ledger abstraction, which attracts the most criticism for its sequentiality. The serial nature not only restricts concurrent consensus instances, but also limits the block validation parallelism. Some research projects aim to replace a linear chain with a direct cyclic graph (DAG). Transactions and blocks no longer need to compete for a single valid position at each height. But more concurrency brings challenges in security, i.e., Byzantine-fault tolerance. How do peers reach an agreement on an identical transaction history out of a DAG, given Byzantines' presence? Below, we draw distinctions between different DAG-styled blockchains, analyzing their features and security implications.

Afterward, we turn around to blockchain state organization. Section 1.1 shows that the unique Bitcoin transaction structure tracks the cryptocurrency flow, up to the point where they are minted. Though real identities are hidden behind public keys, cryptocurrency provenance still conveys abundant information. This motivates a number of interesting data mining research. Researchers perform explorations on the Bitcoin ledger and other similar cryptocurrencies. From another perspective, they can be regarded as concrete attacks on Bitcoin's privacy. It helps understand blockchain security by analyzing their approaches and insights. At last, we investigate improvements in authenticated data structures. These improvements are necessitated by the utility expansion of smart contracts and blockchains.

3.3.1 Ledger Abstraction

DAG-styled blockchains generalize conventional blockchains by allowing a block to reference multiple predecessors. Blocks at the same height no longer need to contend for a single slot. Learned from [277], we classify DAG-styled blockchains based on two perpendicular dimensions. The first is on the nature of DAG nodes, i.e., whether they are batches of transactions (`block-based`) or a single transaction (`blockless`). Blockless can be considered as a special case where blockchain protocols impose a single transaction per block. The second dimension is on the ledger topology and has a cardinality of three. Protocols of `Convergent` blockchains specify totally ordered nodes out of the DAG, which are deemed as decided. This is as opposed to `Divergent` ones where decided nodes only exist in partial orders. Unlike the above, DAGs in `Parallel` blockchains are limited to the form of multiple chains. Despite a variety of structures, each peer replicates the entire ledger, instead of a ledger fraction. Below, we use an example to analyze each design, especially its security implications.

Block-based versus Blockless The initial rationale for Bitcoin to batch transactions into blocks is to amortize the cryptographic operations, i.e., in the PoW consensus. But with the advent of more efficient consensus, drawbacks of block-based designs overshadow their benefits. For example, batching drags on transactions, which is particularly unfavorable to the EOV paradigm. Longer delay increases odds that transactions' read records are modified by others before their validation. Staled reads render them aborted under EOV. This concern on latency motivates EOV Streamchain to remove blocks and directly operate on transactions [170].

Blockless designs are especially attractive in DAG-styled blockchains. In the ledger, the pointers of a block's predecessor are dependent on internal transactions. Consider a block with a transaction that reclaims the cryptocurrency protected in another block. Then the former block must point to the latter to acknowledge the causal order. More transactions in a block incur more causal constraints, thereby limiting concurrency opportunities. This explains why blockless designs are desired in Divergent DAG-styled blockchains. These blockchains are born to reduce unnecessary ordering.

Convergent. DAG-styled blockchains featured for Convergence attempt to establish a total order of DAG nodes, authoritative for agreements between peers. Conflux is one of the typical block-based platforms [189]. As illustrated in Fig. 3.7a, block edges in Conflux belong to two types, parent or reference edges. A block contains a single parent but may have multiple references to others. With only parent edges considered, Conflux first derives a pivot chain with the Ghost protocol. Each pivot block in the chain occupies a unique height. For each height, the pivot block along with its reachable blocks share the same epoch. The reachability takes into account both parent and reference edges. Conflux specifies the below rule to determine the total order of blocks. Blocks are first ordered by their epochs. Within each epoch, blocks are then topologically sorted in a deterministic manner.

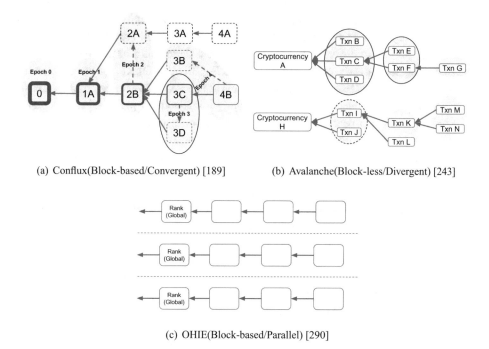

(a) Conflux(Block-based/Convergent) [189]   (b) Avalanche(Block-less/Divergent) [243]

(c) OHIE(Block-based/Parallel) [290]

Fig. 3.7 Diverse ledger shapes in DAG-styled blockchains. **a** Conflux differentiates between parent (solid arrow) and reference (dashed arrow) edges. Ghost protocol establishes Pivot blocks (blue) with only parent edges considered [263]. At each height, a pivot block together with its reachable blocks constitutes an epoch. Both edge types can contribute to reachability. Conflux derives a total block order first by sorting based on their epochs and then topological order within each epoch. **b** Avalanche organizes transactions that redeem the same output as a conflict set (in gray). For each conflict set, Avalanche employs a consensus instance to agree on the single winning transaction. Transactions are non-ordered if they deal with disjoint cryptocurrencies. **c** The ledger of OHIE consists of parallel chains. The Rank field in a block facilitates the establishment of a total order for all blocks despite being in different chains

The Conflux paper extensively proves its safety. But its convergence behavior is far trickier than expected. For example, [290] demonstrates a concrete Byzantine attack on Conflux. The attack could prevent rule-following peers from converging into consistent block order. In reality, the lack of security plagues most Convergent, DAG-styled blockchains. It is due to a fundamental conflict between the DAG-provided flexibility and the total ordered requirement. With the presence of Byzantines, these would pose tremendous challenges to system robustness.

Divergent. Divergent blockchains no longer demand a global order. Instead, they rely on application specifics to extract independence. For example, blockless Avalanche exploits the cryptocurrency flow structure [243]. Avalanche groups all transactions which redeem the same cryptocurrency as a conflict set. A conflict set is marked in gray, as shown in Fig. 3.7b.

Each conflict set embodies a consensus instance to resolve a single winning transaction. Conflict sets may be independent, like the ones with the solid and dashed border. This is because they pertain to different cryptocurrencies. But there could be another story when transactions operate on the same cryptocurrency. In Fig. 3.7b, the fates of the two conflict sets with solid borders are intertwined. Another notable aspect is that Avalanche employs a novel consensus approach. In particular, peers randomly initialize their preferred transaction in each conflict set. Then, a peer repeatedly samples neighboring peers for their preferences and aligns its own to the majority choice. Provided with enough neighbors and a minor fraction of Byzantines, the majority-following rule can effectively mask misconduct. And a peer's updated preference will in turn persuade others. Through herd effect, protocol-following peers are steered toward a common outcome.

Divergent DAG-styled blockchains are featured for their on-demand convergence, where the exact demand is defined by the applications. Avalanche is centered on a cryptocurrency application. It enables Avalanche peers to agree on a number of monetary flows. Different flows work on disjoint cryptocurrencies. Their independence brings much efficiency and simplicity. However, such restrictions impose obstacles to the wider applicability of Avalanche and its alike. Consider contract-enabled blockchains with custom programmability. The conflict domain of their transactions is not so well-defined as in cryptocurrencies. A contract-invoking transaction can be arbitrarily complicated. Intuitively, it may involve multiple conflicts and induce massive constraints. All such complexities could stand in the way of the adoptions of Divergent DAG-styled blockchains.

Parallel. Ledgers of the aforementioned blockchains are in form of natural expanding DAGs. Their protocols leave much flexibility for blocks or transactions in their predecessor references. Compared to them, Parallel DAG-styled blockchains impose a more restrictive ledger format. Their ledgers are strictly structured in parallel chains. Each chain alone is not much different from traditional blockchains. But protocols may mandate chain-specific eligible conditions on their transactions. For example, all the transactions in a chain have to operate on an address range. Transactions may be partitioned into chains by their hashes. A Parallel DAG-styled blockchain can be simply seen as several concurrent chain instances. This simplicity makes them amenable to formal proofs originally proposed for conventional blockchains. This security analysis, such as the one in Sect. 3.1.1, is rigorously established. It is in contrast with the previous DAG-styled blockchains, which must undertake error-prone reasoning from the scratch.

Though Parallel blockchains could inherit most of the security arguments from conventional blockchains, they are inevitably equipped with cross-chain coordination. This coordination brings security challenges and overheads. Let us take the example of OHIE, a block-based platform where transactions are hash partitioned [290]. All OHIE block have a rank, as illustrated in Fig. 3.7c. The rank globally orders blocks even across chains. Given OHIE's total ordered nature, the coordination places overhead on the chain synchronization. Particularly, before a block in a chain is decided, it must wait to ensure that no blocks in other chains could be sequenced ahead.

Summary. In this section, we review the features and security of DAG-styled blockchains. We note that our classification method is based on [277]. Our analysis is limited to a few exemplified systems. Interested readers may refer to Table 2 in the original paper for an exhaustive coverage [277]. Or, readers may delve into papers for their exact protocol designs and justifications.

3.3.2   State Organization

Transaction Analysis. There is an intriguing paradox in permissionless blockchains. They employ cryptographic techniques to hide the real identities of transacting users. But their publicly available ledgers also give power to investigators to perform in-depth analysis. Below, we summarize a few research that move against anonymity. Precisely, they perform data mining on ledgers to unveil user patterns and discern insights. But before that, let us refresh on the Bitcoin UTXO transaction structure, a reiteration of Sect. 1.1. A transaction is made up of inputs and outputs. An output associates a cryptocurrency amount with a snippet of the protective script. The output script usually involves a public key hash as a recipient address. And it encodes signature verifications on future input-provided parameters. An input references the output of a previous transaction. It also attaches script-required parameters to unlock the output-protected cryptocurrencies. In a nutshell, a Bitcoin transaction redeems from previous transactions' outputs. Then, it encodes the transfer to recipients in its own outputs.

The transaction-encoded linkage information makes it possible to derive a complete transaction graph. We draw an example in Fig. 3.8a. In the graph, nodes and edges represent transactions and monetary flows, respectively. Researchers also transformed the transaction graph into an address graph [244], as shown in Fig. 3.8b. Nodes and edges in an address graph correspond to addresses and transactions, respectively. In addition, researchers merge addresses as long as these addresses appear to be senders of the same transaction. As these addresses are jointly manipulated, they are assumed under the control of the same user. Given this, researchers further contract the address graph to an entity graph. And they conclude that the wealth concentration in Bitcoin is more prominent than previously expected.

Bitcoin does not come with its own user directory. Nevertheless, there are plenty of authenticated users with their addresses disclosed, i.e., to accept payments. It opens up chances to integrate the external scattered information into the analysis. In [239], researchers annotate transaction graphs with these disclosed identities. This enables them to partly track the subsequent flow of an alleged Bitcoin theft. In [280], researchers feed the complete transaction graph into machine learning models, intending to classify transactions' legality for Anti-money Laundering. In light of the ledger de-anonymization risks, [149] proposes metrics to evaluate users' privacy. For instance, in their definition, a user's anonymity degrades with more frequent address reuses. Then they conduct their evaluation on the Bitcoin ledger to reason on users' behavior. Similar ledger explorations also prevail on Ethereum [123, 161].

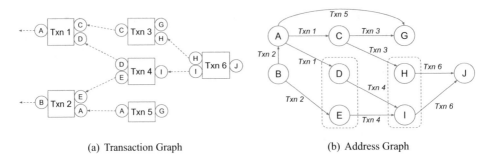

(a) Transaction Graph   (b) Address Graph

Fig. 3.8 An example of a Bitcoin's transaction graph and the corresponding address graph. **a** The Bitcoin ledger natively encodes a transaction graph. In this graph, nodes are transactions and edges represent the redemption of address-bound cryptocurrencies. **b** A transaction graph can be transformed into an address graph. Then transactions become edges and nodes become addresses. Reference [244] further transforms an address graph into an entity graph. An entity graph merges addresses on inputs of the same transaction to a single entity. As enclosed in dash boxes, Txn 4 merges Addresses D and E, and likewise Txn 6 for Addresses H and I

The Ethereum ledger additionally provides contract invocation patterns as another source of interest [122]. Beyond transactions' anonymity, their parallelism is being of independent interest [240, 254]. This is inseparable from the blockchains' shifting bottleneck toward execution. The parallelism level determines the maxed-out speedup.

State Integrity. A Merkle tree underpins the state integrity of contract-based blockchains. Verkle tree is a recent Merkle tree improvement [183]. It attempts to reduce the proof size and accelerate proof generation. Beyond blockchains, verifiable databases also use similar data structures for state verification. Given this ubiquity, ForkBase natively embeds a POS Tree [194, 278]. A POS tree provides similar verifiability functionality and it is more balanced compared to a Merkle tree. ForkBase can relieve applications of tedious and error-prone developments to build a Merkle tree on top of flat storage. This saving in development efforts is empirically shown in [246]. In this work, the researchers replace the original blockchain storage with ForkBase. On top of it, they continue to build a Merkle DAG that captures state evolutions and dependency. As such, the integrity guarantee extends from the latest states to the entire data provenance. A Merkle DAG allows smart contracts to access provenance information in a trustworthy way. This effectively expands on blockchain utilities, as contracts can now encode enriched, history-dependent logic.

3.4   Sharding

Distributed databases pioneer sharding for scalability. This technique partitions data into disjoint shards and manages them independently. By spreading the workload, more computing resources are expected to scale up a system volume ad infinitum. Blockchains are known for their low performance. Bitcoin's throughput remains constantly low, despite that more computing resources (miners) are pouring in over the years. Blockchains are gathering momentum in the industry. But their unsolved problem of scalability is getting amplified. And naturally, researchers attempt to explore database-inspired sharding, so that blockchains can also reap the benefits of horizontal scalability. Naively, peers are grouped into a number of smaller-size committees to process workloads in parallel. But compared to databases, the presence of Byzantines brings many unexpected intricacies to blockchains. As we demonstrate in Sect. 2.5, with a smaller size, Byzantines could collude to infiltrate a single committee. With data partitioned, a single corrupted shard would completely wreck a system.

In this chapter, we study the security issues that sharded blockchains may confront, and the mitigation of these road bumps. Firstly, we examine scalability based on the Blockchain Trilemma. This Trilemma imposes a two-out-of-three design decision which no conventional blockchains could stave off. After the classification of existing blockchains according to their flavors, we motivate why sharding is heralded as a key solution for blockchain scalability. Secondly, a prominent issue of secure blockchain sharding is on the shard formation. In particular, each peer committee shall reflect an accurate statistical representation of the population. By bounding the Byzantine fraction to an eligible threshold, efficient state-machine replication can be applied to each committee. Internal peers can then reach a Byzantine-tolerant agreement on their in-charge partial states. We take a deep look at the vulnerabilities and their remedies during the shard formation. Thirdly, cross-shard transactions are inevitable in sharded blockchains. We show that some cross-shard coordination methods share a similar spirit with a Remote Procedure Call (RPC) and the Two-phase Commit (2PC) in databases. However, they may entail subtle differences due to their distinct data models. As we will see later, cryptocurrency blockchains with the UTXO data model can safely rely on transaction senders to act as quasi-2PC coordinators. Some other blockchains must elect a root committee for the duty. At last, we dig into Atomic Cross-Chain Swap (ACCS). ACCS is a coordination task that enables asset exchanges across blockchains and among mutually distrusting participants. We regard the Atomic Cross-Chain Swap as a specific instance of cross-shard transaction, where a shard amounts to a stand-alone blockchain. Unlike sharded blockchains, whose committees are homogeneously set up, any cross-chain operations, including ACCS, have to overcome the heterogeneity of the involved chains. To address this heterogeneity, ACCS relies on the notion of asset ownership and accompanied incentives for participants. To shield the heterogeneity, several standards on the blockchain behaviors and message patterns have come forward to facilitate the exchange of values and information.

3.4.1 Blockchain Trilemma and Sharding

The Blockchain Trilemma comes from a heuristic generalization of Vitalik Buterin, the founder of Ethereum [77]. Vitalik criticizes a fundamental trade-off that no conventional blockchains can escape: only two properties out of decentralization, scalability, and security can be simultaneously achieved. These properties are defined below.

- **Decentralization.** Blockchains shall eliminate centralized control and distribute responsibilities over a network of homologous peers.
- **Scalability.** Blockchains are capable to process a growing volume of workloads.
- **Security.** Blockchains shall withstand attacks and robustly deliver services.

The Trilemma provides a novel viewpoint on blockchain scalability. Figure 3.9 illustrates the Trilemma with example blockchains in their positions. Bitcoin and Ethereum exemplify the category that focuses on decentralization and security. In these conventional blockchains, which are mostly PoW-based and single-chain, added resources serve to beef up the platform security. For example, Byzantines need to expend proportionately to subvert the longest chain, in an attempt to revert the already-committed transactions. But these extra resources do not contribute to scalability. The consensus protocols dynamically adjust the mining difficulty to keep unchanged performance-related parameters, such as block intervals. Permissioned blockchains sacrifice decentralization in favor of scalability and security. Their throughput can reach thousands of transactions per second, with the Byzantine-fault tolerance guaranteed by state-machine replication. However, they must operate under a limited scale, usually below hundreds of peers. This is incomparable to tens of thousands in Bitcoin. The DAG-styled blockchains and the deployments with multiple independent chains occupy the last edge of the triangle in Fig. 3.9. They focus more on decentralization and scalability.

Fig. 3.9 The blockchain Trilemma and blockchains with their flavors. PoW-based blockchains sacrifice scalability for security and decentralization. Permissioned blockchains favor scalability and security. Despite scalability and decentralization, the security provision of DAG-styled blockchains is not as strong as for the other two categories

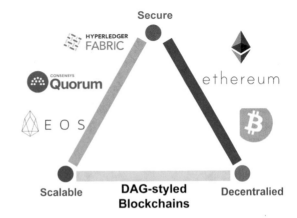

Their security is neither rigorously established nor empirically tested compared to the other blockchains.

The proponents of sharding believe the technique achieves a comfortable sweet spot to resolve the Trilemma. Sharding groups peer into a number of committees. Each committee independently runs the consensus to validate transactions from one of several chains or a portion of a single chain. Committee peers' signatures can serve as a transaction validity proof throughout. The security of the whole blockchain is then collectively guaranteed by committees. Sharded blockchains can admit more peers to increase decentralization. The uptick in peers also translates into more committees. And more committees linearly scale up the performance due to parallelism. But there is a notable distinction between sharded and parallel blockchains. Parallel blockchains are a subclass of DAG-styled ones, as mentioned in Sect. 3.3. In sharded blockchains, peers may hold a partial view of system states. In parallel blockchains, the complete ledger is fully replicated in each peer. In the light that each peer must perform validation and consensus on all transactions, parallel blockchains exhibit zero scalability.

3.4.2   Shard Formation

We further break down blockchain shard formation into the below three sub-problems. During the discussion, we may reference some non-sharded blockchains, such as Algorand [153] and Byzcoin [177]. Even though they only elect a single committee, they also pertain to the discussed issues.

Peer Selection. Peer selection aims to pick qualified representatives to form committees. For selected peers to statistically reflect the population, permissionless blockchains must defend against Sybil Attacks. Forging identities shall not increase Byzantines' likelihood to get elected. To this aim, Eth2 [30] and Algorand [153] employ PoS. Byzcoin [177], RapidChain [293], Omniledger [178], and ELASTICO [201] utilize PoW. In their designs, peers must produce a valid solution to become qualified. The targeted difficulty functions are described in Eqs. 3.1 and 3.2. Underpinned by the unpredictability of hash functions, Byzantines and non-Byzantines find no better-off ways other than randomly sampling for solutions. Peers' solutions can then reflect their dedicated computing resources or staked cryptocurrencies. Algorand replaces hash functions with Verifiable Random Functions (VRF, as detailed in Appendix A.1) for its PoS-based peer selection [153]. As an asymmetric-key version of a hash function, the exact function differs between peers by their private keys. This further strengthens the unpredictability of the peer selection outcome— Byzantines cannot reason about others' VRFs.

Delegated Proof-of-Stake (DPoS) resembles real-world democratic elections [22]. In EOS, peers set up their delegates by casting their votes to show their confidence [25]. Votes take the form of staked cryptocurrencies. The top-voted delegates are qualified for committees. For all sharded permissioned blockchains, we observe none of them entail peer selection [87, 132, 133]. All peers participate in the committee formation.

Committee Formation. The above procedure bounds the Byzantine fraction of the selected peers as in the entire population. But when grouping peers into committees, Byzantines could exploit the lineup to dominate a committee. To fend off the unevenness, sharded blockchains rely on a random seed to power the distribution. Moreover, they make a stronger assumption about the population's Byzantine fraction t. The assumption is more conservative than the tolerance level f from their committee consensus. For example, ELASTICO [201] and Omniledger [178] assume $t = 1/4$ as they use PBFT with $f = 1/3$. RapidChain [293] and AHL [133] are modeled with $t = 1/3$ as $f = 1/2$ in their consensus protocols. Conditioned on the unpredictability and unbiasedness of randomness, this extra margin can limit the likelihood of a compromised committee, by enlarging the committee size. A committee is compromised when its internal Byzantine fraction is more than f. The exact probability is formulated as a cumulative binomial distribution, in particular,

$$P_{byzantine\_comm\_permissionless}(n; f, t) = \sum_{x=\lceil nf \rceil}^{n} \binom{n}{x} t^x (1 - t)^{n-x},$$

where n is the number of peers in the committee. When $t < f$, careful inspection may reveal that $P_{byzantine\_comm\_permissionless}$ exponentially diminishes to being negligible, with an increasing n. Further, given m committees, a system failure rate is then bounded by the union $P_{byzantine\_system\_permissionless} = m P_{byzantine\_comm\_permissionless}(n)$. Given this, protocol designers can tune m and n for the performance-security trade-off. Similar reasoning can also apply to permissioned blockchains, except that their probability of a Byzantine committee follows the hypergeometric distribution. Particularly, with a total population of $N = nm$ and at most $\lfloor tN \rfloor$ Byzantines, the probability of a Byzantine-dominated committee can be computed as

$$P_{byzantine\_comm\_permissioned}(n; f, t) = \sum_{x=\lceil nf \rceil}^{n} \frac{\binom{\lfloor tN \rfloor}{x}\binom{N-\lfloor tN \rfloor}{n-x}}{\binom{N}{n}}$$

The countable nature of permissioned membership accounts for this difference. In permissionless blockchains, peers are selected from an infinite population. It implies whether a peer in a group is Byzantine does not impact the Byzantine likelihood of others, i.e., they are fixed to t. Their committee formation is analogous to sampling with replacement. On the other hand, hypergeometric distribution describes a sampling process without replacement. It is because the total population in permissioned blockchains is limited, and the probability of an assigned peer being Byzantine depends on the other peers.

Now, we describe how to seed the required randomness for an even committee formation. Byzantines bring challenges to the unpredictability and unbiasedness of distributed randomness generalization. Considering F Byzantines, a strawman design would dedicate each of

$F + 1$ peers to contributing one portion of a random secret, aggregating them, e.g., by concatenating them, and then using the aggregated secret to drive the committee formation. The above scheme takes into account at least one non-Byzantine peer, where the unpredictability and unbiasedness come from. However, this approach is security flawed. Consider the following attack where the other F Byzantines could wait until the only non-Byzantine reveals its random portion. Then, they would selectively choose their own secrets to bias the final result. An immediate remedy is to protect secrets via security commitments. Peers hide them until all $F + 1$ peers finish the commitments. Then, they disclose their secrets to aggregate the final. This enhancement prevents Byzantines from adaptively changing their committed secrets. However, Byzantines could refuse the disclosure and indefinitely postpone the process. They may do so because the non-Byzantine's disclosed secrets are not favorable to them. In this light, a more robust approach is to replace the security commitments with Verifiable Secret Sharing (VSS) [72]. VSS allows each peer to compartmentalize its secret and distribute distinct portions to others. Notably, the peers' actions to separate and disseminate a secret are verifiable. And a peer's secret can be recovered when enough recipients make public their allocated shares. By decentralizing the secret recovery instead of a single-point disclosure, VSS prevents Byzantines from biasing the aggregated randomness. RandomHound is a distributed random-generating scheme designed in this spirit. But it comes with an additional focus on message reduction. Many sharded blockchains employ RandomHound and alike for Byzantine-resistant randomness [178, 293]. Apart from this, some blockchains create their own schemes and prove the security individually [30, 153, 177, 201]. The most idiomatic one is AHL [133]. Researchers delegate the seed creation to a Trusted Execution Environment (TEE) [69], which relies on hardware vendors to uphold randomness. With a secure random seed, committee grouping rules are intuitive. ELASTICO [201] includes the seed as an input of the PoW function, during the peer selection. Successful miners are lined up according to their PoW nonces, i.e., peers in the same committee share an identical suffix pattern [201]. Omniledger [178] and AHL [133] partition peers based on a permutation uniquely computed from the seed. Likewise, RapidChain constructs a randomized bipartite graph, which links peers to committees [293].

Committee Reconfiguration. Committees require periodic reconfiguration in sharded blockchains. This is to prevent slowly adaptive Byzantines. These adversaries can leverage the transparent assignment setup and flexibly migrate their powers to corrupt peers, compromising the committee security. However, the attacking procedure is assumed to take time. Otherwise, no committee arrangements could withstand instant corruption. Slow adaptive Byzantines necessitate sharded blockchains to adjust their committees by epochs. From a security standpoint, an epoch length accommodates for Byzantines' corruption speed. It also balances the reconfiguration frequency, one of the performance factors.

Though exact reconfigurations differ between sharded blockchains, their distinctions are nebulous. ELASTICO [201], Omniledger [178], AHL [133], and Algorand [153] fully re-elect committees between epochs. At the end of an epoch, peers generate randomness to seed the next-round peer selection and committee formation. Among them, Algorand [153] takes the most conservative assumption on Byzantines' adaptivity. It only allows one block per epoch, while others' epoch length may be in the range of hours. RapidChain [293] and Byzcoin [177] are featured for a partial swap. They use the above shard formation technique for a trustworthy committee bootstrap. Then they perform partial committee adjustments across epochs. For example, Byzcoin [177] sticks to the round-robin manner. A newly selected peer with a PoW solution kicks out the eldest one from the committee. At any moment, the committee constitution proportionately reflects the peers' possessed powers within the most recent time window. As a consequence, the Byzantine fraction in the committee is always bounded.

3.4.3   Cross-Shard Transaction

With committees robustly set up, blockchains can partition system states to shards and assign data shards to committees, i.e., by partitioning record key hashes. However, under partitioned states, cross-shard transactions could go wrong under Byzantine attacks. Section 2.5 describes how fragile they are. A misbehaved 2PC coordinator could easily fool shards by equivocating transaction status. This breaks atomicity as transaction updates could be partially committed in shards. In the following, we explain how sharded blockchains withstand Byzantines for cross-shard transactions. We generalize their approaches into the following three categories. The first one is cross-shard invocation which achieves per-transaction atomicity while forgoing intertransaction Serializability. The second approach is inspired by Two-phase Commit (2PC) in databases which preserve both atomicity and Serializability. The third category sidesteps all these partition-induced problems. It does so by establishing a total order for all committee-validated transactions.

Cross-shard Invocations. Cross-shard invocations aim to invoke a transaction in one shard/committee with references to states or transactions in another one. It can be implemented with cross-shard messages or sender-relaying transactions. Both are respectively shown in Fig. 3.10a, b. Cross-shard messages in sharded blockchains behave like Remote Procedure Calls, where the caller and callee are both committees. This brings challenges to the message reliability and integrity under Byzantines attacks. For example, the presence of Byzantines rules out the design to designate a single peer as the sender or recipient for its committee. The message could carry $F + 1$ peer signatures to attest its authenticity (F is the number of Byzantine peers). But the sender or recipient peer could remain non-responsive to indefinitely postpone the delivery. Reference [165] delves into protocols for robust, cross-shard message delivery. In a nutshell, the protocol prescribes one-to-one correspondences between peers in sending and receiving shards beforehand. A Byzantine-resistant message delivery must be backed up by $F + 1$ matching correspondences.

Some sharded blockchains abandon complicated cross-shard messages. In turn, they rely on transaction senders (clients) for the relay of cross-shard invocations. RapidChain [293] and Monoxide [276] are two examples of sharded cryptocurrency platforms. They both parti-

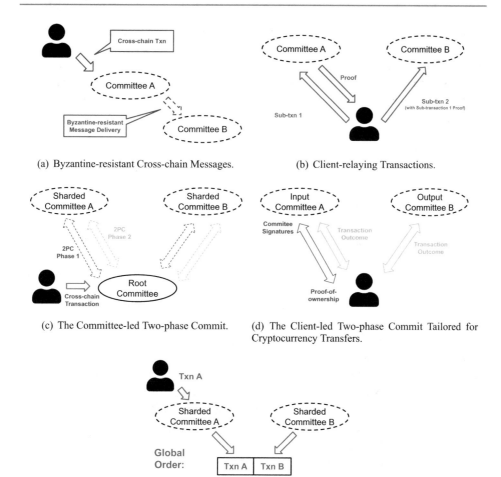

(a) Byzantine-resistant Cross-chain Messages.

(b) Client-relaying Transactions.

(c) The Committee-led Two-phase Commit.

(d) The Client-led Two-phase Commit Tailored for Cryptocurrency Transfers.

(e) A Global Order from Committee-validated Transactions.

Fig. 3.10 Paradigms for cross-chain transactions. **a** A cross-chain Remote Procedure Call is achieved with the Byzantine-resistant Cross-chain message delivery. **b** A cross-chain transaction is split into sub-transactions, to be relayed by transaction senders driven by their incentives. **c** A root committee drives the Two-phase Commit (2PC) to coordinate sharded committees for cross-chain transactions. **d** A transaction sender (client) serves as the 2PC coordinator for its cryptocurrency transfer. **e** A sharded blockchain establishes a total order from independently committee-validated transactions to arbitrate conflicts

tion states based on payment addresses. To achieve a cross-shard transfer, RapidChain [293] requires the client to break it into two sub-transactions. The first transfers cryptocurrencies to the committee in charge of the recipient, but still under the client's control. The second sub-transaction finalizes the transfer inside the committee. Similarly, Monoxide [276] breaks a transaction into withdrawal and deposit operations. A client must first commit the withdrawal to the source committee, marking the source cryptocurrency as spent. Only with the withdrawal proof from the committee, the sender can go for the deposit operation in the recipient committee. Eth2 generalizes the above relay mechanism to generic smart contracts [30]. A shard may refer to another shard state during its transaction execution. But the state references must be accompanied by a committee-attested Merkle proof for their integrity.

The security of client-relaying transactions is not technically guaranteed as the committee-led cross-shard messages. The atomicity can still be justified by the user's rationality. For instance, in Monoxide [276], it is possible that a client performs withdrawals but without deposits. But this would render its cryptocurrencies locked and result in an unfavorable situation. Driven by incentives, a rational client would refrain from leaving cryptocurrency transfers halfway. Unlike cryptocurrencies, incentives in smart contracts are not well-defined. It requires contract developers to align incentives with respect to the interest of contract users. When users always find themselves in a better-off position after the execution, they can be incentivized to behave honestly, i.e., not to halt the transaction halfway.

2PC and Its Adaptions. Cross-shard invocations achieve transaction atomicity either through Byzantine-resistant message delivery or by users' incentives. However, they may compromise Serializability due to an unpredictable gap between sub-transactions. Consider the following non-serializable scenario when records A and B are partitioned. Both start with value 1, before they undergo two cross-shard invocations T_{add} and T_{mul}. T_{add} increments both values by 1 and T_{mul} multiplies them with 10. Suppose in the middle of T_{add} when A has incremented to 2 but B remains 1, T_{mul} updates $A = 20$ and $B = 10$. After T_{add} finishes its last part to increment B, the final effect $A = 20$, $B = 11$ does not correspond any serialized effect of T_{add} and T_{mul}.

In reality, Serializability plagues transactions not only in blockchains but in databases. In the latter, the issue is mitigated by Two-phase-Commit (2PC). The crux of 2PC is to add a tentative phase before transaction updates actually take place. Specifically, in the first phase, a transaction coordinator instructs shards to hold locks on updated states, if they are not already locked. If the coordinator is aware that some updated states have been locked previously, the coordinator in the second phase would inform all shards to do the rollback and release the locks. Otherwise, on the occasion when the coordinator acquires all the locks, the coordinator would inform shards to effectuate the updates. Explicit locking remedies the above-described situation, i.e., a transaction intrudes on another one's execution.

Some sharded blockchains idiomatically follow the 2PC paradigm. For example, to fit into the decentralized setting, AHL hardens 2PC by replacing the single-point coordinator with a root committee [133]. As illustrated in Fig. 3.10c, the root committee coordinates sharded committees, the counterparts of 2PC participants in databases. In a word, AHL implements 2PC on top of Byzantine-resistant state-machine replication. 2PC state transitions, such as locking data and determining transaction outcomes, must undergo the consensus of sharded committees and root committee, respectively.

The support of generic workloads results in excessive complexities in AHL, when AHL attempts to secure 2PC on top of Byzantine-resistant state-machine replication. But for Omniledger [178] and RSCoin [132], their restricted focus on cryptocurrencies and the simplicity of the UTXO data model can bring convenience. Let us refresh on the unique structure of cryptocurrency transfers in Fig. 1.1 and Sect. 1.1, particularly what inputs and outputs are in the UTXO data model. If we treat a cryptocurrency transfer as a normal transaction with data updates, its updates shall consist of both inputs and outputs. Outputs create addresses and associate them with cryptocurrencies and spendable conditions. Inputs mark their referenced outputs as redeemed, a state modification to prevent duplicated spending. Thereby, in a sharded cryptocurrency platform, a standardized 2PC shall involve both inputs and outputs in each of the two phases. However, Omniledger and RSCoin completely skip outputs in the first phase. Instead, a transaction sender, as the coordinator, only informs input-corresponding committees of a potential transfer and collects spending qualifications from them. Then, in the second phase, the user sends all the collected qualifications to the involved committees to confirm the transfer. Outputs are then generated in the second phase.

The relieved concern on outputs in the first phase can be explained due to the non-contention nature of outputs. Outputs are considered distinct. Though different outputs may relate to the same address, it is regarded that an owner possesses two different spending sources. Due to the distinctness, outputs are guaranteed to be conflict-free. No transfer could be aborted due to the contention on outputs. Thus, it finds no necessity to lock-protect them in the first phase. Besides the saving efforts on outputs, the UTXO data model brings another benefit. Clients can safely operate as 2PC coordinators for their own transactions. This single-point design can be similarly justified by clients' economic incentives, just like client-relaying transactions as above. Technically, a client could instruct shards to mark their inputs as redeemed, but without creating outputs. Factually, it would break the transaction's atomicity. But rational transaction clients refrain from doing so. It is because they would get their balances frozen, contrary to their best interest. The client-led, cryptocurrency-tailored 2PC is drawn in Fig. 3.10d.

Merging Sharded Transactions. Regardless of cross-shard invocations or 2PC adaptions, the transaction coordination is on a demand basis. Sharded blockchains optimistically assume that transactions operate on disjoint data shards and run them independently across committees, except when they access states on a common partition. Another, more pessimistic approach is to merge all the transactions into a total order, despite that they are independently validated by committees. We illustrate this paradigm in Fig. 3.10e. The global order can be leveraged by applications to resolve conflicts for coordination. To establish the global sequence, GeoBFT mandates that committees must advance in rounds [162]. For each round, a committee must wait for others to complete before going forward. At the end of a round, each committee must learn about the consensus-decided transactions from all the others. Then, the transactions are deterministically ordered, e.g., by their hashes.

Elastico favors a more centralized design [201]. A final committee is designated to run a Byzantine-tolerant consensus to agree on the global order. Compared with the traditional single-chain design, peers in the final committee only need to verify committee signatures for transactions' validity, without re-executing them. An order-dependent coordination can proceed as follows. Suppose A is an unspent transaction output. Two transactions $A \rightarrow B$ and $A \rightarrow C$ both attempt to spend it. Due to the parallelism, the two transactions pass the validation on two different committees. Suppose a global sequence places $A \rightarrow B$ ahead of $A \rightarrow C$, an application-imposing rule can treat the latter as invalid. Another benefit of the total order is that workloads need not be state- partitioned. The goal of state partitioning is to provide a coarse-grained way to identify conflicts and coordination needs. Apparently, this is not necessary under a pessimistic global-ordering approach. Blockchains could blindly assign transactions based on their hashes to committees. They can do so without inspecting transactions' accessed states and other semantics.

It is not without downsides to use a global order for coordination. Most intuitively, this needs synchronization between all committees in GeoBFT [162]. Elastico's approach is worthwhile only when the committee signature verifications take less time than re-executing the transactions [201]. When blindly partitioning workloads, vacuous transactions may be another issue that wastes the system's volume. Or they can be exploited by Byzantines which could bias the global order. Due to the presence of Byzantines, the final committee cannot determine a canonical state during the consensus. Hence, it is impossible to build a Merkle tree to guarantee state integrity. (Traditional blockchains with the Execute-order-validate paradigm are also prone to a similar problem. As discussed in Sects. 3.2.2 and 3.2.3, their transactions are subject to aborts after the ordering/consensus.) In this light, Elastico retains state partitioning, i.e., cryptocurrency inputs determine responsible committees. In this way, transactions which spend the same sources will always be processed by the same committee. This eliminates vacuous transactions, as any potential conflicts will be resolved before establishing the global order.

3.4.4 Atomic Cross-Chain Swap and Blockchain Interoperability

Atomic Cross-Chain Swap (ACCS) allows mutually distrusting participants to exchange cryptocurrencies on heterogeneous blockchains [6]. We treat ACCS as a special instance of cross-shard transactions, where each shard is a stand-alone blockchain with its own participants, transactions, and states. As involved blockchains operate in silos and are not aware of each other, we do not have the luxury to rely on Byzantine-resistant cross-chain messages. Consider a simple scenario where Alice has Bitcoins and Bob has Ethers, Ethereum's native cryptocurrency. Both intend to exchange their holdings, but they do not trust each other. Nor do they believe in any intermediaries or escrows. The decentralized setting brings many difficulties. First of all, if both participants do the transfer in sequence, the first mover is at a disadvantage. Suppose Alice first transfers her Bitcoins to Bob. Bob could refuse to go for the Ether transfer, rendering Alice at loss. A seemingly effective remedy is to require both participants to submit transactions simultaneously. But this remedy is by no means

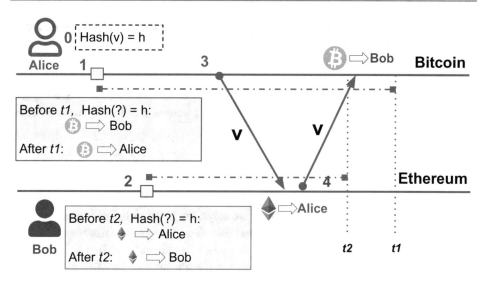

Fig. 3.11 Atomic cross-chain swap between mutually distrusting Alice (with Bitcoins) and Bob (with Ethers). (0) Alice privately generates a random string v and computes its hash h. (1) Alice commits a Bitcoin transaction, which encodes its recipient Bob's spending condition: provide a value with hash h. Another condition imposes that, if Bob does not do so before time $t1$, Alice will get her Bitcoins back. (2) Bob gets to know h and $t1$ from Alice's committed transaction, but he is not aware of v. Bob commits a similar transaction on Ethereum. Likewise, it encodes the transfer of Ethers to Alice only provided with the correct solution before $t2$. Time $t2$ must be earlier than $t1$. (3) Once aware that Bob's transaction is committed, Alice commits a v-inclusive transaction to redeem Bob's Ether before $t2$. (4) The above transaction exposes v. The difference between $t2$ and $t1$ enables Bob to create a similar Bitcoin transaction with v to redeem Alice's Bitcoins

robust. Both Ethereum and Bitcoin employ a PoW consensus, which does not guarantee finality and may result in unpredictability. It is possible that Alice's transaction resides in a shorter, to-be-pruned chain, while Bob's transaction takes effect in the longest chain. Then Alice refuses to redo the transfer, rendering Bob at loss. If one understands how tricky an ACCS is, she would better appreciate the solution illustrated in Fig. 3.11. In a nutshell, the protocol leverages Bitcoin scripts and Ethereum smart contracts to encode additional spending conditions for recipients. At each step, participants would find it better to take the protocol-prescribed action, rather than deviating from the protocol. Participants are driven by their incentives to coordinate, ending up in an atomic transfer. At the outset, Alice privately prepares a random string v and its hash h. Then, the protocol proceeds as follows:

1. Alice commits a Bitcoin transaction, which encodes Bob's spending condition: provide a value with hash h. If Bob does not do so before time $t1$, Alice gets her Bitcoins back.
2. After Alice's transaction is committed, Bob gets to know h and $t1$ from Alice's transaction, but is not aware of v. Bob commits a similar transaction on Ethereum. Likewise, it

encodes the transfer of Ethers to Alice only provided with the correct value v before $t2$. Time $t2$ must be earlier than $t1$.

3. When Bob's transaction is committed, Alice commits a v-inclusive transaction to redeem Bob's Ether before $t2$.
4. The above transaction from Alice exposes v on the Ethereum ledger. The period between $t2$ and $t1$ enables Bob to create a similar Bitcoin transaction with v to redeem Alice's Bitcoins.

We assume that $t1$ and $t2$ are long enough such that transactions in Steps 3 and 4 will definitely commit within the interval, for example, by repetitive requests. We informally justify why the above protocol guarantees security, i.e., the atomicity of the exchange. If either Alice or Bob fails to follow the first two steps, the other participant would regard it as an unwillingness for the coordination, and thus abort the process. Atomicity does not break as there is no transfer at all. Unless Alice behaves honestly in Step 3, Bob cannot lose his Ethers. In the meantime, Bob cannot get Alice's Bitcoins as Alice would at best protect her private value v. If Alice and Bob choose not to collaborate until $t1$, both can get their cryptocurrencies back, without breaking the atomicity. Let us assume that Alice honestly reclaims Bob's Ethers with v before $t2$. This step discloses v to Bob. With v, Bob has the incentive to take Step 4 to get his exclusive Bitcoins from Alice. More importantly, Alice is incapable to prevent Bob from doing so. It is because Alice's transaction (for Bob's conditional spending) has been committed on the Bitcoin chain. It is done in Step 1, earlier than Step 4. Alice cannot revert the action due to the blockchain's immutability. Careful reasoning would reveal why Bob is inclined to set $t2$ earlier than $t1$ for his interest. The difference between $t1$ and $t2$ provides a safety margin for Bob's countermeasures. Think from the other way around, when $t1$ is earlier than $t2$. Then protocol-deviating Alice would get her Bitcoin back immediately at $t1$. At any moment later than $t1$ but before $t2$, Alice could still gather Bob's Ethers while Bob cannot take any counteraction.

The above ACCS protocol entails two participants and has four sequential steps. Reference [166] generalizes the problem for more participants and wider transfer patterns. In particular, the problem is modeled as a directed graph G, with participants as nodes and transfers as edges. The author concludes that a protocol exists for ACCS if and only if G is strongly connected. Afterward, given a qualified G, the author proposes a protocol that takes D steps. D is the diameter of G. Reference [292] assumes that blockchains could reference each other. For example, the Ethereum contract can verify in a trustworthy way the presence of a Bitcoin transaction. Given this, researchers propose an ACCS protocol, inspired by 2PC. In the protocol, the number of sequential rounds is always bounded to two despite the complexity of G. In the above, intended transfers in an atomic swap are all unconditional. ACCS fails to consider the scenario when Alice wants to transfer to Bob only when she receives the payoff from Carol. Reference [167] incorporates conditional transfers, augmenting Cross-Chain Swap to Cross-Chain Deal. Cross-Chain Deal provides an enriched abstraction to structure commercial interactions.

Blockchain Interoperability. ACCS and its outgrowths spearhead the strides toward a landscape of interoperable blockchains. But heterogeneity remains a major stumbling block. As we have seen, ACCS overcomes this by defining and leaning on the abstraction of hash-protected and time-bound transactions. It does not concern how individual blockchains implement these abstractions. Despite this, incentives for mutually distrusting participants ride on these abstractions to govern their asset exchanges. However, when it comes to broader value-exchanging applications or even arbitrary cross-chain interactions, the above approaches would definitely fall short, as no well-defined ownership notion can be leveraged. Worse still, a growing number of siloed blockchains further contribute to the fragmented sphere [136]. And this fact itself comes as a morale-sapping acknowledgment of the dimming prospect for a one-size-fits-all blockchain [9]. To boost blockchain interoperability, researchers aim for a higher abstraction level, by extracting more commonalities among a diversity of blockchains. Their efforts come with a slew of standards specifying system state transitions and message patterns, in order for the governed blockchains to speak a common language. Notable specifications include Polkadot XCMP [49], Cosmos IBC [16], and Interledger Protocol [268]. However, in their competition for a TCP/IP's equivalent in the blockchain realm, we haven't observed any of them claim the top spot. Beyond data standardization, this vision paper discusses more challenges in blockchain interoperability [136].

3.5 Layer-2 Scaling

Layer-2 approaches are another way to scale up blockchains while guaranteeing security. Unlike sharding, we do not find related techniques in databases for Layer-2 approaches. Nor can we locate their position in our taxonomy of distributed transactional platforms. The essence of a Layer-2 approach is to offload the bulk of multi-party coordination off the chain. The chain only reflects the pre-execution and post-execution states. Besides that, the blockchain serves as a mediator in case of misconduct among mutually distrusting parties. Rational participants are aligned to behave honestly in their best interest, even though their actions are conducted off the chain. Non-compliant participants are subject to countermeasures from the compliant ones and punishment from the blockchain. Since Layer-2 only requires a total of two transactions on the ledger, applications could reach potentially unlimited throughput with ample out-of-band communication. Beyond the infinite scalability and the instant finality, off-chain transactions save transaction fees for users and better protect their privacy.

In this chapter, we first present a technique known as Payment Channels to demonstrate the power of off-chain mechanisms [48]. Our example exhibits secure unidirectional cryptocurrency transfers between two mutually distrusting participants. It is specifically tailored for UTXO data models. We then shed light on how to turn Payment Channels bidirectional, extend for arbitrary parties, and generalize for state-based contracts. We regard Sidechains as specific instances of Channels [98]. A Sidechain requires participants to arrange the off-the-main-chain transactions into a stand-alone entity. A Sidechain is periodically synchronized with the main chain. This facilitates the settlement of misconduct of sidechain's participants. At last, we examine a Layer-2 construction that is used in Ethereum, Rollups [113]. Rollups enable a designated participant, a relayer, to roll up transactions from transactors for local, in-batch execution. The relayer reflects the post-execution condensed results on Ethereum's main chain. The relaying transaction also provides bare-minimum proofs of execution correctness.

3.5.1   Channels

Payment Channels on cryptocurrencies resemble membership schemes in commercial practices. A loyal consumer could work with a retailer and pre-deposit an amount of money in a membership card, analogous to opening a channel. They also negotiate an exit scheme to withdraw the balance. Future consumption could be directly debited from the membership card, without going through cash or external banking services. This is just like the later-mentioned transactions off the chain. However, such a scheme endows too much trust on retailers, as they could technically block card usage. Fortunately, Payment Channels are out of this concern, as the blockchain serves as a trustworthy arbiter. Below, we use a classic Alice-and-Bob example to demonstrate the Payment Channel in Bitcoin, as shown in Fig. 3.12a. In terms of the above analogy, Alice corresponds to the consumer and Bob to the retailer.

Unidirectional Payment Channel. For the initialization and close-down of channels, Alice and Bob jointly prepare Txn1 and Txn2 with the following format. Txn1 transfers 10 Bitcoins from Alice to a multi-party address, to be spent when both the signatures of Alice and Bob are used. Txn2 redeems the Bitcoins from Txn1 with their joint signatures and credits them to Alice. Notably, Txn2 is specially coded to be considered valid only one week after Txn1 persists its effects on the chain. The commit of Txn1 signals the initialization of the payment channel between Alice and Bob. The 10 Bitcoins and the one-week period are the channel capacity and the validity period, respectively. They are respectively equivalent to the deposited amount and date-of-expiry of the membership card. Alice holds Txn2 privately, without committing it on the chain. Txn2 serves as the means of exit for Alice to withdraw her balance. For a transfer, Alice and Bob can perform the following off-chain action as follows. Alice locally prepares a half-signed transaction that spends the unique output of Txn1, and redistributes the amount accordingly. For example, Txn3 reflects a Bitcoin transfer from Alice to Bob. Noticeably, the transaction is signed only by Alice, and it is handed over to Bob, with Bob's signature blank. Once Txn3 is within the possession of Bob, both participants, especially Bob, can safely regard that the transfer has finished. The entire procedure can be done off the chain, as Txn3 does not need to be committed. But what is the impact on security? From the recipient standpoint, Bob only needs to make

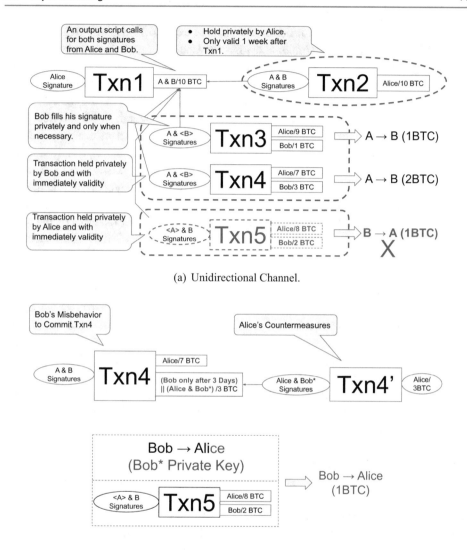

(a) Unidirectional Channel.

(b) Revocable Transactions for Bidirectional Transfers.

Fig. 3.12 Cryptocurrency payment channels. **a** Alice and Bob open a channel having a capacity of 10 Bitcoins and a period of 1 week. They do so by jointly preparing Txn1 and Txn2, with Txn1 committed on the chain and Txn2 kept by Alice locally. Alice locally prepares a half-signed Txn3 and hands it over to Bob. This marks a credible 1-Bitcoin transfer from Alice to Bob. Similarly, Txn4 marks a 2-Bitcoin transfer. However, Txn5, which attempts a backward transfer, is non-credible to Alice. **b** Revocability requires tweaking Bob's output of Txn4. It can either be redeemed by Bob 3 days later when committing Txn4, or Bob*, another address of Bob, can do so immediately. To revoke Txn 4, Bob should surrender Bob*'s private key to Alice. In doing so, Alice can rest assured of Bob's possession of her non-favored Txn4. If Bob maliciously commits Txn4 to the chain, Alice could counteract by committing Txn4'. Txn4' can immediately reclaim Bob's output with Alice-possessed Bob*, earlier than any redemption from Bob, which is possible only 3 days later

sure to sign Txn3 and commit it before the channel expires. He has the right incentives to do so for his interest. More importantly, Bob understands that Alice's possessed Txn2, even though not in his favor, could only take effect 1 week later. Given that Alice cannot prevent Bob from reclaiming his portion during the channel validity period, Bob can believe in the fate of the transfer. In a likewise fashion, another offline Txn4 can be coined to mark a subsequent transfer of 2 Bitcoins from Alice to Bob. Even though Bob holds both Txn3 and Txn4, Bob will favor the latter as Txn4 is more financially attractive. Alice could not prevent Bob from committing Txn4, before the channel expires. However, can we similarly coin a subsequent transaction that attempts a backward transfer? This is like Txn5, which aims to send one Bitcoin from Bob to Alice. Intuitively, Alice cannot accept the transfer. It is simply because Alice knows Bob's possession of Txn4, which reflects a non-favored position to herself. If Bob commits Txn4 to persist the pre-transfer balances on the chain, there are no countermeasures from Alice to safeguard her interest. Given this, the backward transfer is non-credible. The above explains why the flow of the above payment channel is limited to one direction.

Revocable Off-chain Transaction. Evidently, if we want to support bidirectional transfers, we must add a revocation mechanism. This must allow a participant to revoke an earlier off-chain transaction. Moreover, it must persuade the other party to do the revocation. Taking the above example, Bob shall revoke Txn4 and Alice shall be persuaded. Then, the backward transfer from Txn5 is capable to gain its credibility from Alice. In Fig. 3.12b, we explain how to make Txn4 revocable in a trustworthy way. The spending condition of Bob's output in Txn4 is tweaked into a disjunction of two. Either Bob could unlock the protected Bitcoins with his exclusive private key but 3 days later, or the Bitcoins can be immediately claimed with a joint signature from Alice and Bob*. Bob* is another address whose corresponding private key is initially kept by Bob. The revocation of Txn4 can be manifested by the surrender of Bob*'s private key to Alice. With Bob*'s private key, Alice reassures the credibility of Txn5. The credibility stems from her potential countermeasures to Bob's misbehavior. For example, consider that Bob maliciously commits Txn4 in a bid to nullify the backward transfer. Upon the observation of Txn4, Alice can generate a counter-transaction Txn4' with both signatures from her own and Bob*. Then, Txn4' could instantly drain Bob's portion to Alice's pocket. Bob could not prevent Alice's counteractions, as his spending condition is 3 days after Txn4.

This paragraph only explains the necessity and efficacy of off-chain transactions with revocability. Revocable transactions are core enablers to bidirectional payment channels. However, a full-fledged design considers more subtleties than that. For example, a bidirectional channel must be designed with symmetry. The above does not account for Alice's revocability, clearly a lack of consideration. We direct the readers to this lecture note for more details [224].

Lightning Network and State Channel. Now, we present how to support payments from arbitrary parties and generalize this to state-based smart contracts. Lightning Network aims for the former [236]. It allows two mutually distrusting participants to transact without explicitly setting up a channel. Both participants rely on relays. In particular, Lightning Network is a loosely connected graph of peers. Each pair of peers set up a bidirectional channel. Peers and their connections form the backbone of Lightning Network. A sender and a recipient shall at first identify a path of peers. Their transfer is then separated into several off-chain mini-transfers. Peers in the path sequentially relay the mini-transfers along. And Lightning Network provides a reward mechanism to incentivize peers for the correct behavior. Similar to Atomic Cross-Chain Swap in Sect. 3.4.4, the mechanism is necessary for transaction atomicity.

For generic contract support, State Channel augments the concept of Payment Channel. State Channels are implemented on smart contracts, unlike Payment Channel on UTXO data models. Despite this, State Channel shares a similar spirit with the latter. During the opening phase, two participants, Alice and Bob, shall work together and lock some states on a contract, e.g., their assets. Additionally, they pre-agree on an anti-dispute mechanism, to be encoded and enforced by contracts as well. The mechanism allows any participants to single-handedly invoke the contract, so that they quit with their assets unlocked. But the unlocking must take a long enough time, for the other party's awareness. With this mechanism, participants can conduct the state-modifying operations off the chain. During the process, consider the occasion that Bob attempts to unlock his assets by referencing an outdated state. The outdated state allows Bob to reclaim more. Upon Alice's observation, she could immediately file a complaint with proof of her latest possessed state. Alice's proposed challenge would undergo verification from the contract. If the contract verifies that Bob maliciously committed an invalid state, the contract would enforce the punishments on Bob. For example, Bob's locked assets would be credited to Alice. At any time, Alice and Bob can jointly invoke the exit means in the contract. Then, assets are immediately unlocked and fairly redistributed.

3.5.2   Sidechains

Sidechains put in place the Channel idea in a constrained context [98]. In particular, participants maintain an independent child chain (`sidechain`) with off-the-main-chain operations. The block digest of the child chain periodically synchronizes with the main chain. The digest helps the arbitration in case of misbehavior from the child chain participants. Let us examine a concrete example. Plasma is a Sidechain solution for Ethereum [235]. Alice and Bob rely on Plasma to resolve instant Ether transfers, as shown in Fig. 3.13. At the outset, Alice and Bob together create a Plasma contract on the Ethereum main chain. Each of them deposits five Ethers for the contract custody. They also set up a child chain. Its genesis states are initialized with the deposited amounts in the main chain. Then Alice and Bob can transact on the child chain, without burdening the main chain. In Fig. 3.13, Alice and Bob make two subsequent transfers. Periodically, the Plasma contract in the main chain is informed about child block header hashes. These hashes provide condensed information

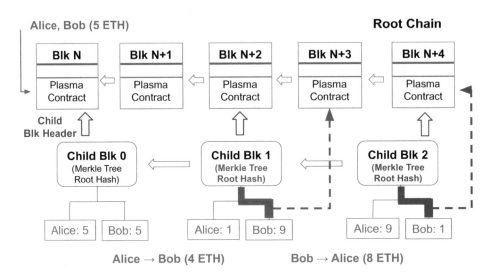

Fig. 3.13 Plasma, a sidechain solution on Ethereum. Each of Alice and Bob deposits five Ethers to the Plasma contract on the main chain. They also set up a child chain that is initialized with their deposited balances. Alice and Bob then transact on the child chain. The child block hash is periodically submitted to the Plasma contract in the main chain. Suppose that Bob maliciously produces an outdated Merkle proof and invokes the Plasma contract, as an attempt to reclaim his balance (colored in red). Alice could submit a fraud proof (colored in blue), a Merkle proof on the latest balance of Bob. Then the contract would impose penalties on Bob

about the child chain. At any moment, either participant can invoke the Plasma contract for a request to exit with the locked Ethers. But he/she must provide a proof with a block header and Merkle path. The proof attests that he/she possesses assets in the side chain. The exit request is subject to challenges for a period of time. If the other participant submits a fraud proof, the exit request is considered invalid, and the Plasma contract would impose punishments on the requester. In the example of Fig. 3.13, Bob intentionally fouls the main chain with an attestation on his outdated balance. In doing so, he could reclaim more Ethers, despite that he has made a transfer to Alice. During the challenge period, Alice could file a fraud proof on the latest balance of Bob. The Plasma contract performs the verification and imposes the penalty on Bob.

When compared with Channels, Sidechains and Plasma offer more benefits. They reuse existing techniques to secure off-the-main-chain transactions. These techniques, such as the blockchain consensus and Merkle paths, are established and less error-prone. This is opposed to Channels, which call for a robust analysis of incentives and a careful craft of schemes. Secondly, Sidechains are capable to scale when only a few parties are involved. The scalability depends on their child consensus. The game design in Channels is only fit for two participants. Thirdly, Sidechain is amenable to hierarchy. While the main chain works as the arbiter of a second-layer chain, the second-layer chain then arbitrates a third-layer chain. If the second layer chain is corrupted, a third-layer participant could bring upward their fault proofs to settle the request in the main chain. This resembles leveled courts in a judicial system.

3.5.3 Rollups

Channels enable two mutually distrusting parties to credibly transact off the chain. Sidechain applies off-chain communication to a federation. Nonetheless, as both techniques follow a check-and-balance paradigm, they cannot escape the following fundamental downsides. First of all, security hinges on the full-time availability of participants. In the Plasma example of Fig. 3.13, suppose Alice is offline during a period longer than the challenge window. Bob could exploit Alice's negligence for his misconduct, leaving no room for the former's counteractions. Secondly, a key driving force of check-and-balance mechanisms is incentive-powered actions from rational participants. But except for a few classic use cases with strong notions of ownerships, participants' incentives are hard to define. Or, it requires substantial application-specific reasoning.

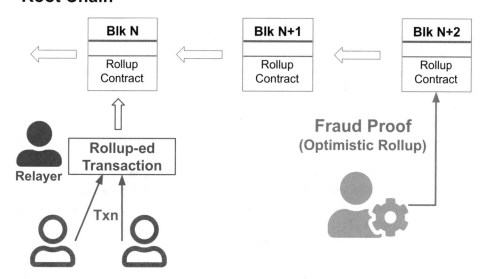

Fig. 3.14 Rollup, the state-of-the-art layer-2 technique on Ethereum. A relayer collects transactions and runs them locally in a batch. The relayers prepare a single transaction that reflects on the post-execution states. The transaction is submitted to the Rollup contract in the main chain. Under Optimistic Rollup [46], the correctness of relayers' transactions is subject to challenges by fraud proofs

Given the above shortcomings, the Ethereum community nowadays heralds Rollups as a general-purpose Layer-2 technique [113]. Rollups are capable to simulate the full Ethereum environment. In Rollups, any user could deploy a Rollup contract with their staked cryptocurrencies on the main chain. They can then assume the duty of relayer. Relayers collect transactions from transactors and run them locally in batch mode. Relayers send a rollup-ed transaction to the contract. A single transaction contains the post-execution states in their compressed form. From the perspective of transactors, relayers are trust-free, as their local executions are subject to verification. The verification differs between Optimistic Rollups [46] and ZK-Rollups [78]. The former follows a conventional check-and-balance mechanism. Relayers' behaviors are assumed correct until the contract receives their fraud proofs. Relayers' stakes would be slashed as a penalty. In the latter, Rollup-ed transactions contain a succinct cryptographic proof called a ZK-SNARK [78]. ZK-SNARKs (Succinct Non-interactive ARgument of Knowledge) enable relayers to make publicly verifiable their local execution and availability. Magically, ZK-proofs do not leak any data or computations. ZK-SNARKs are an advanced cryptographic technique that is theoretically intensive. Even Rollups in Ethereum are currently still in their infancy. Hence, we only briefly present their basic ideas, as summarized in Fig. 3.14.

3.6   Summary and Further Reading

In this chapter, we attempt to draw a complete landscape of the latest blockchain research. We present the latest works according to the four layers in our taxonomy, as defined in Chap. 2. In general, researchers work on either of two challenges, (i) how to strengthen blockchains' security or (i) how to boost up their performance without compromising the security.

One line of attempts at Replication is on the formal modeling of Proof-of-Work (PoW), the soul of Bitcoin. Particularly, researchers transform PoW into a classic Byzantine-tolerant protocol that satisfies Safety, Liveness, and Validity. The discovery of Selfish Mining further necessitates the need for an established formalism, as these tricky mining policies would cause an unfair distribution of compensations. Many researchers improve the PoW mechanism to make it faster, greener, or more usable. The rise of blockchains also triggered a resurgence of conventional state-machine replication to achieve Byzantine-fault tolerant consensus. We group these consensus protocols into three categories, Partial Synchronous, Synchronous, and Asynchronous protocols. The classification is based on how they sidestep the FLP Impossibility [148].

Conventional blockchains follow the Order-execute paradigm. Though they stick to the serial nature for ease of understanding, their contract behavior is far finickier than expected. More importantly, blockchain immutability makes impossible any vulnerability-patching mechanism, rendering risks particularly acute. It is especially the case in Solidity-coded contracts in Ethereum. We exemplify three contracts, each showing a vulnerability from one of the three categories, `Language-level`, `Runtime-level`, and `Platform-level`. Many preventions and impediments come to the rescue for Order-execute blockchains, in a bid to make their contract behavior more predictable. Transactions in blockchains of the Execute-order-validate (EOV) paradigm carry their invoking effects to shrug off any ambiguity. But the EOV paradigm may abort in-ledger transactions, a performance issue that attracts the attention of database researchers. Several proposals are hybrids of two paradigms, for their joint benefits.

On blockchain storage, a ledger provides a canonical history of transactions. But its sequentiality imposes performance bottlenecks. Several blockchains explore alternative designs. They allow a child block to reference several parents, thus forming a DAG-styled ledger. Some systems even abandon the block-batching design and operate at the granularity of transactions (`blockless`). We line up DAG-styled blockchains into the below three categories. The `Convergent` category attempts to establish a global order of blocks/transactions of a DAG ledger. The `Divergent` category exploits the application semantics for a partial order. The `Parallel` category consists of blockchains that are structured in several parallel chains. For each group, we use an example to lay out designs in concrete forms. We also shed light on the security challenges for Byzantine tolerance. We include several data mining research on the blockchain ledger, from the consideration of attacks on privacy. Enhancements on the Merkle tree are also of independent interest in this chapter. These authenticated data structures are vital to guarantee state integrity.

At a glance, sharding in blockchains seems to be similar to its counterpart in databases, but it is in fact fundamentally different. We first motivate sharding based on the Blockchain Trilemma. Though promising, the presence of Byzantines brings forward a variety of security problems. To defend against Sybil Attacks in permissionless blockchains, selected peers shall reflect the accurate statistical characteristics of the population, so as to bound the Byzantine fraction. To evenly group peers into committees, sharded blockchains demand a secure random generation in the distributed fashion. Slow adaptive Byzantines warrant the periodic committee re-formation. With committees formed and data partitions assigned, cross-shard transactions could be another issue. We classify cross-shard techniques based on two orthogonal dimensions. One dimension is whether the control flow is unidirectional (`Cross-shard Invocations`) or not (`Two-phase Commit and Its Adaptions`). The other dimension is whether the coordination hinges on a transaction sender or a designated root committee. The sender-led coordination is mostly seen in cryptocurrency blockchains with the UTXO data model. This data model brings many simplifications to its tailored Two-phase Commit. Apart from the above design flavors, there exist sharded blockchains that resolve coordination with a global order from all sharded transactions. Finally, we examine the Atomic Cross-Chain Swap, an instance of cross-shard interaction targeting asset exchanges between stand-alone blockchains. We generally remark that blockchain interoperability targets more generic interactions.

We suggest that readers with a background in databases should pay special attention to Layer-2 approaches in blockchains. We single them out as we do not find similar techniques

Table 3.4 Blockchain surveys

Layer	References
Replication	[103, 108, 225, 279, 284]
Concurrency	[95, 120]
Storage	[196, 231, 277]
Sharding	[96, 197, 274]
Blockchain Interoperability	[105, 184, 294]
Layer-2	[157, 158, 259]
Other	[126, 137, 191, 193, 299, 300]

in databases to scale up services. Layer-2 ramps up the blockchain volume by offloading the bulk of traffic off the chain. The credibility of off-chain transactions is underpinned by a check-and-balance mechanism among mutually distrusting participants. We use a `Unidirectional Payment Channel` as an example. We further extend it for bidirectional transfers with `Revocable Off-chain Transactions` that support arbitrary transactors with `Lightning Network` and the applicability for contracts with `State Channels`. Sidechains are a special implementation of State Channels, where a child chain batches all the off-the-main-chain transactions. As we have seen in Ethereum's sidechain Plasma, Merkle Proofs help to identify Byzantines' fraudulent actions. At last, we summarize Rollups, which is heralded as Ethereum's next-phase scaling approach. When compared with Channels and Sidechains, Rollups is more generic and does not require participants' full-time participation.

In the end, for comprehensiveness, we compile recent blockchain surveys in Table 3.4.

Blockchain Applications 4

In the previous chapter, we reviewed the latest technical progress in blockchains. We discussed works whose goals are to improve the security and performance of the blockchain systems. Another parallel line of work is to find new applications for blockchains that are beyond cryptocurrencies. Such efforts involve developing smart contracts for existing and new use cases.

In this chapter, we draw a global picture of blockchain applications. In particular, we choose four representative domains. They are finance, supply chain, healthcare, and identity services. For each area, we explain use cases that highlight the disruptive potential of blockchains. Throughout the discussion, we bear in mind the following general questions:

1. How are applications technically grounded in blockchains?
2. What are the distinctive advantages blockchains can offer, when compared with traditional database-powered approaches?
3. What are the challenges and issues in their deployments?

4.1 Finance

Blockchains are born to facilitate currency transfers. Hence, extending blockchain usages to financial services is natural and straightforward. One basic application is `tokenization`. It allows users to create their own representations of the value and to securely transact. We differentiate between fungible and non-fungible tokens, and we discuss how they are supported in Ethereum contracts. Decentralized exchanges enable token trading in an intermediary-free way. We use the `Automatic Market Maker` (AMM) for illustration. AMM leverages smart contracts to facilitate trades with trust and transparency. Decentralized exchanges are only a foundational infrastructure of decentralized finance, but not the whole. We then draw

© The Author(s), under exclusive license to Springer Nature Switzerland AG 2022
P. Ruan et al., *Blockchains*, Synthesis Lectures on Data Management,
https://doi.org/10.1007/978-3-031-13979-6_4

```
1   contract FungibleToken {
2       // A map from addresses to numeric balances records the amounts of
            fungible
3       // tokens that each holder possesses.
4       mapping(address=>uint256) public balances_;
5
6       function transferFrom(address _from, address _to, uint256 _value)
7           returns (bool success) {
8           // Validate that the invoking transaction is properly signed by
9           // the corresponding private key of _from.
10          if balances_[_from] >= _value {
11              balances_[from] -= value;
12              balances_[to] += value;
13          }
14      }
15  }
```

Listing 4.1 Fungible tokens

a general overview of other financial applications, empowered by blockchains. At last, we conclude with challenges and issues within these use cases.

4.1.1 Fungible and Non-fungible Tokens

Tokens in blockchains are units of value that represent digital or real-world assets. Assets can be tangible, such as cars, houses, and artworks. Digital assets may include money, copyrights, patents, company shares, certificates, and so on. Tokens may also represent the voting power of holders in a decentralized application. Another dimension to classify assets is based on their fungibility. Fungible assets refer to those which are interchangeable and divisible. In a sense, a unit of a fungible asset is equivalent to all other units of the same asset. Money and company shares exemplify this category. In contrast, units of non-fungible assets, or non-fungible tokens (NFT), are unique and atomic, such as artworks and copyrights, among others.

Fungible and non-fungible tokens have different contract implementations. Comparing Listings 4.1 and 4.2, fungible tokens are implemented as mappings from addresses to numeric balances, whereas addresses in non-fungible tokens are associated with token identifiers. Despite the distinction, their transfers must be endorsed by the signatures of the original owners. Given the mass popularity of tokenization and demand for tokens interoperability, the Ethereum community proposes two technical standards, ERC-20 [26] and ERC-721 [27]. They are, respectively, for fungible and non-fungible tokens. Such standard is represented by a Solidity contract interface (functions without implementation, with their specifications). Any user can instantiate such interface, e.g., specifying the total number of available tokens and encoding their transfer conditions. Then, the user needs to deploy the contract on Ethereum to make the token available.

```
1   contract NonFungibleToken {
2       // Non-fungible tokens associate the address of holders with token
3       // identifiers.
4       mapping(uint256 => address) public _owners;
5
6       function transferFrom(address _from, address _to, uint256 tokenId)
7           returns (bool success) {
8           // Validate that the invoking transaction is properly signed by
9           // the corresponding private key of _from.
10          if _owners[tokenId] == _from {
11              _owners[tokenId] = _to;
12          }
13      }
14  }
```

Listing 4.2 Non-fungible tokens

Tokenization on blockchain provides the following benefits. Firstly, it harnesses blockchain-guaranteed security. Asymmetric encryption protects the ownership of tokens. Users are relieved from concerns about Double Spending, thanks to Byzantine-fault tolerant consensus. (Double Spending is a well-known issue that manifests when a user spends the same tokens in two or more transactions.) The ledger provides a trusted source of transfer history. Compared with single-point, database-powered approaches, the usage of blockchain shreds trust and dependence on the centralized administrator. The second benefit of Tokenization on blockchain is censorship-resistance. It particularly applies to Initial Coin Offering (ICO). An ICO is the blockchain equivalent to an Initial Public Offering (IPO). An investment-seeking company issues blockchain tokens to investors. Tokens function as shares, manifesting investors' rights for the company's control or qualifications for dividends. In contrast to IPO, the ICO's entry bar is much lower. A company can simply deploy a contract with the ERC-20 standard and publicly announce the deployed address. Investors then invoke the contract to invest with their cryptocurrencies in exchange for the company-issued tokens. The convenience makes possible to technically sidestep regulatory standards. These regulations may include Know-Your-Customer (KYC) or Anti-Money-Laundering (AML).

4.1.2 Decentralized Exchange and Finance

Cryptocurrency exchanges provide venues for users to transact their cryptocurrencies and tokens. Exchanges can be centralized and decentralized. Centralized exchanges are not much different from traditional stock exchanges. There is a central entity that keeps users' assets in its custody. Trading is reflected on the entity's balance sheet. Users are capable to withdraw their assets according to their book-kept balances. Typical examples include Coinbase, Binance, and so on. Decentralized on-blockchain exchanges are non-custodial.

Assets are always under the manipulation of users' digital signatures. A smart contract is responsible to govern the trading, as we will see later in the case of automated market maker. Another dimension to categorize exchanges is their running paradigm. Order-book-styled exchanges only match requests from users but do not take part in their transactions. They accept from users their purchasing and selling requests with prices and quantities. They make deals when the purchase price is higher than the selling price. In contrast, market-maker-styled exchanges transact on both sides with their offered prices. Besides earning commissions, they can charge a spread on the buy and sell price as compensation for their supplied liquidity.

Now we dive into `Decentralized`, `Market-maker`-type exchanges, which gather momentum with Uniswap [70] on Ethereum. The idea is simple. Let us assume there are an x amount of TokenA and y amount of TokenB in the pool. There is a smart contract that holds amounts of both (ERC-20) tokens. Users can invoke the contract to exchange on type of token for the other. The contract imposes the following constraint before and after the invocation: $x * y = k$, where k is a fixed constant. In this manner, buying or selling actions essentially shift (x, y) along a reciprocal curve. Given the above invariant, a unit price of TokenX, measured by TokenY, is inversely proportional to their pooled amount ratio. For instance, when TokenA outnumbers TokenB, the pricing formula favors the latter. (A unit of TokenB can be exchanged for more than one unit of TokenA.) This would attract users to sell TokenB to the contract. The selling action would ramp up the TokenB amounts in the pool, hence pushing down its price. More importantly, in permissionless Ethereum, the price self-adjusting mechanism is open to users. When the in-contract price is discrepant from the external price, it creates a fair arbitrage opportunity that users can exploit for profits. The arbitrage would drive the in-contract price toward the market. Besides exchanges, users could also deposit (withdraw) both tokens in the contract pool. These actions essentially supply (drain) liquidity and increase (decrease) k. Moreover, liquidity providers are rewarded.

Figure 4.1 illustrates the difference between the aforementioned automated market maker and its centralized counterpart. The former is featured for its accessibility and transparency. In the latter, the pricing mechanism remains a black box to users. With a transparent pricing formula, users are free from the concern of Insider Trading. The service availability of a central entity is not technically guaranteed. However, the traditional approach outperforms the decentralized one in performance and user-friendliness.

Automatic Market Makers, such as Uniswap [70] and Sushiswap [58], stand for the category of Decentralized Exchanges. Decentralized Exchanges are the foundational infrastructure for Decentralized Finance. Beyond these, there are more projects that transform conventional financial products onto blockchains. TomoDEX [66], dYdX [23], and Nash [45] mark attempts on the order-booked decentralized exchanges. Stablecoins aim to ameliorate the fluctuating prices of cryptocurrencies and tokens. They peg the value of the token to fiat cryptocurrencies, commonly the US dollar. Stablecoins can be custodial, such as USDT [60]. A central entity issues tokens backed up by an equal amount of pegged assets in their reserves. The token's price stability comes from the collateralization at the custodians.

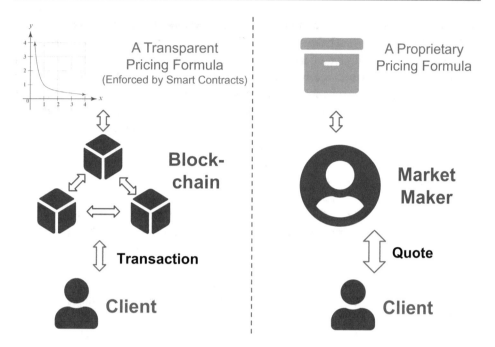

Fig. 4.1 Automatic Market Maker (AMM) versus Centralized Market Maker. While the AMM's price is determined by a transparent in-contract formula, clients have a blind spot on how the centralized market maker sets the price. AMM outperforms the conventional approach on the security, transparency, and accessibility, but cannot rival with the latter on the processing volume

In contrast, non-custodial stablecoins are implemented in a decentralized manner, such as DAI [18]. Their values stem from cryptocurrencies or other valuable tokens collateralized in a smart contract. There is a contract-coded pricing mechanism that algorithmically imposes the price pegging. Compound [14] and Aave [3] are contract-leveraged lending protocols for loanable funds of crypto-assets. Notably, Aave [3] provides a form of uncollateralized loans, termed as flash loans. The lifetime of a flash loan is restricted within a transaction. In a sense, users may borrow crypto-assets at the start of the transaction. But they must repay the amount and interest before the transaction ends. The atomicity constraint is imposed by smart contracts and blockchains. Flash loans provide risk-free funds for traders.

4.1.3 Challenges and Issues

In blockchain-powered financial applications, challenges are always accompanied by opportunities. First of all, trust is not always guaranteed in an end-to-end manner. It particularly applies to blockchain applications that involve real-world assets. Think about the case when a non-fungible token (NFT) represents the ownership of a piece of physical artwork, and the owner loses its possession (e.g., it was stolen). This creates an ambiguity on who is the real owner of the artwork. What happens if the police, a central authority, does not consider the ownership record as reflected on blockchain and refuses to take action? Evidently enough, when tokenizing real-world assets, blockchains only provide a secure means of transfers. But real ownership must hinge on a power-holding authority to uphold. There is a clear unfavorable single-point trust here. The above thinking explains why some NFT holders, after digitally tokenizing their possessed artworks, absurdly burn their physical counterparts [7]. It is for the protection of exclusiveness and scarcity of the artwork.

For fungible tokens, nothing brings more controversies than ICOs. In ICO, there is a fundamental tension between its convenience in crowdfunding and the fraud due to the lack of regulations. The lower entry bar for money-raising makes ICOs rife with scams and crimes. Due to its decentralized nature, if a token issuer runs free, no others could be responsible for the losses. Hence ICO requires investors to exercise a high degree of caution for their investments. But there are numerous successful cases that early ICO investors reap a handsome payoff, far more than that in IPO. For example, Ethereum was born from an ICO which raised more than 3,700 Bitcoins for its start-up grant in 2013 [38]. The mixed sentiments on ICO can also be reflected from its divergent legal status in various jurisdictions [38].

Decentralized exchanges are heavily financially involved. This amplifies both the security and performance problems underneath blockchains. There are a number of security breaches in exchanges due to poorly coded contracts or other factors [1]. We examine smart contract vulnerabilities in Sect. 3.2 and show that miners are capable to selectively include transactions and bias their orders. Miners could exploit this to generate additional revenue, often at the cost of users. Miner Extractable Value (MEV) [76] captures this notion and it is currently under heavy study [131, 237]. Besides security, it is frequently reported that a popular ICO or NFT trading leads to a meteoric rise in transaction traffic [33, 62]. The excessive hype congests the Ethereum network, pushing the transaction fee to rocket high. This motivates several Layer-2 techniques specifically tailored for financial applications [20, 57]. They attempt to offload part of the traffic to off-chain while retaining security with a check-and-balance mechanism.

4.2   Supply Chain

Supply chains are another promising area that blockchains are capable to disrupt. A supply chain is a network of material suppliers, carriers, manufacturers, and retailers. They produce and distribute products to final buyers. Due to its inherent decentralized structure, supply chains are a natural fit for blockchains. More importantly, a supply chain consists of numerous stakeholders. Their conflicts of interest are not rare. To resolve their disputes, blockchains can serve as unified trust-building platforms. And they also provide trustworthy information for end consumers. Below, we use a supply chain tracing query to demonstrate

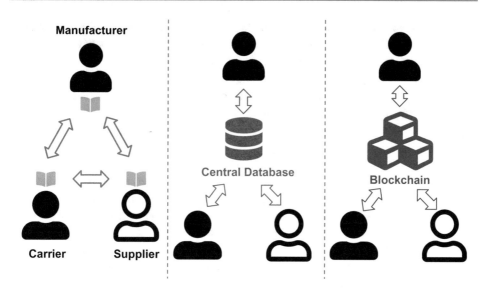

Fig. 4.2 Blockchains for supply chains. (left) Each party independently maintains its fact sheet, rendering supply chain data in silos. (middle) All parties employ a centralized database for the integration. (right) Blockchain provides a unified, trustable platform for transactions and storage

the unique contributions that blockchains offer. Then, we compare it with conventional supply chain management without blockchains. Figure 4.2 draws out their distinctions.

Let us suppose a consumer receives a flawed product. He intends to do a tracing query, so as to find out which party in the supply chain shall hold the liability. In the traditional supply chain, each party independently holds a fact sheet and separately maintains the connections with others. Hence, the supply chain data is fragmented. Then, such a tracing query must be broken down into a number of separate small queries. For example, with respect to Fig. 4.2, a consumer may reach manufacturers to inspect whether the fault is from their side. Or it is due to the damage from carriers and poor quality control from material suppliers. Such recursive procedures require more effort and are error-prone. How about all parties in the supply chain manage a centralized database? The database reflects all relevant transactions and provides a holistic view of the supply chains. This is what some giant companies are doing. For example, Apple is renowned for its supply chain management that regulates downstream companies. However, this single-point approach inherits all the single-point vulnerabilities. The authoritativeness of the central administrator is questionable. This would lead to the trust deficit in its provided data. In the example of Fig. 4.2, suppose that a manufacturer manages the database. Also, assume that the manufacturer shall be blamed for the flawed product. Then, the manufacturer may fake the result and shred its responsibilities to other parties. We can mitigate the data manipulation problem by employing a blockchain instead of the centralized database. A blockchain provides an immutable data repository. All participants share an equal weight of influence on the repository modifications. A blockchain can survive the manipulation from any single point. The blockchain ledger is provenance-friendly, as it encapsulates a history of products and their material sources. The ledger provides a trustworthy source to answer the above tracing query.

There are a few projects that spearhead the initiative to transform the supply chain management with blockchains. Typical examples include Provenance [52] on product traceability. Everledger [63] employs Hyperledger Fabric to track the owners of diamonds. But applying blockchains in supply chains is not without downsides. The most prominent issue is whether blockchain data could faithfully reflect the real-world states. For example, a faulty manufacturer is technically capable to update the blockchain, manifesting that the manufactured product is flawless. The consumer would eventually discover the discrepancy between the purchased product and the blockchain record. But she cannot pinpoint where the fault is. Though the misbehave in data protection can be ameliorated by using automated hardware and sensors, it is questionable whether the data-collecting procedures can be reliably trusted. In [283], researchers provide a simple method to trick these collectors in supply chain management. The other concern is the trust in blockchain vendors. In traditional industries, participants are usually not sufficiently IT-trained. They would blindly utilize the blockchain software supplied by vendors, without knowing what is happening under the hood. Without a solid understanding of blockchain security mechanisms, they would rely much on software vendors. As a consequence, vendors could technically fool them with a fake blockchain, e.g., a blockchain that cannot resist Byzantines. The above two issues are due to single-point trusts in the supply chain applications.

4.3 Healthcare

Just like the supply chain, healthcare is another sector that calls for data integration. It also suffers from a lack of authoritative intermediaries. Think about the frustration of patients, when they have to repeat examinations simply because doctors cannot access previous examinations done in another hospital. Suppose there is a central repository that holds complete longitudinal records. Are their provided data trustable? Who should manage the repository and who guarantees the data accuracy? Worse still, healthcare is a sector with plenty of stakeholders. Insured patients tend to over-claim for more compensation. Uninsured patients have the tendency to downplay their illnesses, to gain bargaining powers for insurance negotiation. Blockchains offer opportunities to consolidate medical records in a trust-free, decentralized manner. Beyond the neutrality in dispute resolution, blockchains have another merit. With cryptographic techniques and ownership proofs, blockchains are capable to put medical records in the hands of their patients. The benefits are two-fold. For patients, the control over their pathological profiles reduces medical paternalism. And so, patients can weigh in more on their own treatments and fates. In the meantime, in the current Big Data era, exclusive data ownership turns medical records into assets. This can unlock vast business

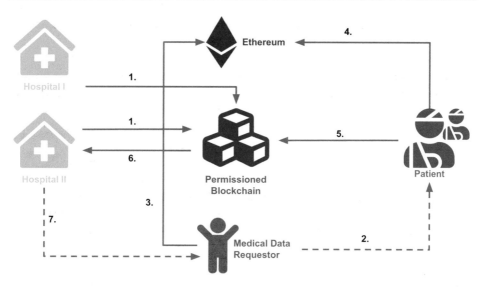

Fig. 4.3 The dual-chain design in Medilot [41], a blockchain solution for healthcare. A hospital updates the digest of a patient's medical record on a permissioned blockchain, leaving the record control to the patient. But the raw record is maintained locally at the hospital side (Step 1). A data requestor approaches a patient off the chain (drawn in dashed line), seeking approval for medical data usage (Step 2). If approved, a patient would reply to the requestor with an Ethereum address. After the patient observes the requestor has made the cryptocurrency payment (Step 3 and 4), she updates the permissioned blockchain with the approval to the requestor (Step 5). The hospital acknowledges it from the blockchain (Step 6) and releases the record to the requestor off the chain (Step 7)

opportunities. The trend is getting prominent, as more AI companies are devoting their efforts to electronic health record (EHR) analysis [117, 261].

In this chapter, we use Medilot as an example to examine how blockchain can revive the healthcare industry's capabilities [41]. We abstract their prototype and summarize their workflow in Fig. 4.3. Medilot is renowned for its dual-chain design which intertwines three classes of stakeholders. They are patients, hospitals (doctors), and data requestors. Data requestors may range from insurance companies, data analysis start-ups, or any institution that intends to collect medical data. Medilot uses two blockchains, Ethereum, a permissionless blockchain, and Hyperledger++, a permissioned blockchain developed by Medilot based on Hyperledger Fabric. Stakeholders with both blockchains run as follows. Per each hospital visit, a doctor will update the digest of a patient's medical record to Hyperledger++. The update links the record digest with the patient's blockchain address. Essentially, it surrenders the record control to the patient. A data requestor approaches the patient and expresses willingness to collect the patient's record with cryptocurrency payments. The patient first acknowledges the cryptocurrency receipt from the data requestor on Ethereum. Then the patient updates Hyperledger++ on his medical record to reflect his consent. The hospital acknowledges the patient's consent from Hyperledger++. Afterward, this hospital releases the patient's medical record to the requestor.

Let us first analyze the benefits of Medilot's dual-chain design. The permissioned blockchain protects the patient's ownership of medical records, a prerequisite for patient-centric care. Unlike a centralized database, no one may find edges to compromise the service or tamper with the data. The ledger provides a unique verifiable transparent source of truth on record ownership, as well as an intermediary-free way to integrate medical data. Besides, the on-chain digest protects patient privacy, as the complete medical record is protected at the hospital side. However, several challenges remain open. Particularly, the trust is not infinite. First of all, just like in the supply chain, healthcare users may not be sufficiently IT-trained. This may require excessive trust in blockchain software vendors. Likewise, stakeholders shall believe in the good faith of data suppliers. Secondly, there are some underneath trusts during the stakeholders' cooperation. For example, what if the patient declines to grant consent on permissioned blockchains even though the requestor has paid on Ethereum? In a similar vein, what if a hospital refuses to release medical records despite that the hospital acknowledges the patient's consent? The former problem involves atomic modifications on two chains. Cross-chain techniques in Sect. 3.4.4 may provide potential solutions. The latter is bundled with stakeholders' off-chain actions, i.e., releasing medical records by hospitals. Legislation can kick in to enforce on stakeholders. But the trust is then delegated to jurisdictions, a centralized authority.

4.4   Identity Management

Identity management (IDM) is another sector where blockchains exhibit their disruption. IDM comprises processes to identify users so that they can be granted privileges for actions and services. Authentication refers to the proving process on properties about a user's identities, such as name and gender. Identity management and authentication are well-established topics. Whenever we access a web service, keying in our username and password is often the first required step. Password checking is a basic form of IDM. Besides, IDM can find its significance in background checking, know-your-customer procedure, and so on. If one has ever been plagued by onerous management of a slew of accounts, we do not need to argue more on how fragmented the current landscape is. The federated approach alleviates the burden by delegating the authentication to an authority. But the convenience is at the expense of excessive dependence on an intermediary. Blockchain-powered self-sovereign identities achieve a perfect sweet spot between them. Users keep full control over their credentials. A blockchain ledger acts as a verifiable data registry, a phonebook that anyone can consult.

Figure 4.4 draws out the distinction between the three IDM approaches. In the server-centric approach, each company maintains its own user credentials. Upon a user's login, they perform independent authentication to establish identities. The drawback is evident. Users have to juggle between various identities across different websites. The federated approach

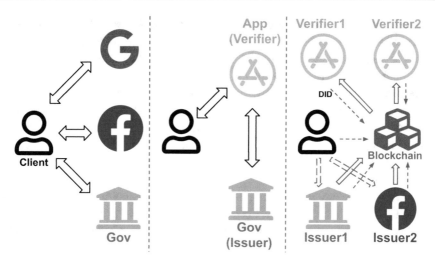

Fig. 4.4 Identity management approaches. (left) In the conventional stand-alone approach, each institution separately maintains users' identities and performs authentication. (middle) In the federated approach, identification requests from small-scale applications (verifiers) are outsourced to an authoritative institution (issuer). (right) In the self-sovereign identity management, each party registers their own decentralized identifiers (DID) on blockchains. DIDs are protected with their private keys. Issuers and verifiers produce and validate DID credentials on a blockchain. The blockchain ledger acts as an open verifiable identity registry

seemingly makes life easier, by delegating IDM to an authoritative third party. For example, many websites allow users to log in with Google accounts. In a sense, Google serves as a credential issuer for authentication, whereas the web service is the verifier. Yet, such a centralized method renders risks particularly acute. The access loss of the Google account may implicate all relevant services. Likewise, a data breach in a central authority may exert a far-reaching impact. In the self-sovereign identity management, all participants, including users, issuers, and verifiers, can create their identities on a blockchain. Their identities are linked with their public keys. Hence, they can be manipulated by their corresponding private keys that should always be kept private by the users. Users may approach any issuers to attest identity-bound facts or properties. Issuers create the credentials signed by their own private keys. Issuers update credentials to a globally accessible blockchain. Users may reference their on-chain credentials for verifiers. Verifiers can then validate the attestations endorsed by issuers.

One may find some resemblance of the self-sovereign identity management with the traditional Certificate Authority (CA) scheme on the Internet. Both serve the same goal to establish identities and authenticate. But they differ essentially in their architecture. The former is decentralized, whereas the latter is centralized or hierarchical. Specifically, in the CA scheme, the authoritative powers of certificate issuers are inherited from their parent authorities. The trust is recursively attributed to the top root authority, a single point of failure.

There are cases where some Certificate Authorities abuse this trust [73]. In contrast, the self-sovereign IDM democratizes the procedure. Any user can generate their own identities and approach any issuers for verification. A blockchain serves as a transparent, intermediary-free platform to facilitate access to credentials.

Nevertheless, some may raise concerns over the arbitrariness of the scheme, as anyone can work as an issuer. It may leave their attestations not as trustworthy as before. As a consequence, verifiers shall exercise a higher degree of caution. When verifying the claim, they must factor in the reputation of the issuer and their own judgment of the issuer. An immediate remedy is to build a reputation system with blockchains. Issuers must stake cryptocurrencies and their issued certificates shall carry the stake proof. In this way, issuers are incentivized to behave in good faith to avoid their stakes being slashed. Their reputation can build up based on their honesty. Correspondingly, issuers can charge more to users or verifiers for their reputed services. In Ethereum, there exists a paid naming service that allows users to create identities [24].

4.5 Summary and Further Reading

In this chapter, we select four representative industrial domains where blockchains have shown their potential to revolutionize. In the financial sector, we show how to tokenize digital or physical assets on blockchains, so that their ownership can be safely transferred. Blockchain contracts enable Automatic Money Maker. Users can swap tokens with a transparent pricing formula. With their decentralized nature, blockchains provide a fair means to integrate data from mutually distrusting sources. They also provide a source of truth to settle their disputes. This particularly appeals to supply chain management, where many stakeholders are involved and conflicts of interest are common. Beyond anti-dispute capability, the provenance-friendly ledger stores the traces of products. The product provenance is amenable to verifiable queries. In healthcare, Medilot shows its attempt to consolidate medical records and capitalize on their values. There are two key enablers. First, a blockchain brings an intermediary-free platform. Second, cryptographic techniques secure the record ownerships. Similarly, with blockchains, identity management and authentication services are democratized with self-sovereignty. In this case, a blockchain serves as a public-accessible verifiable identity registry.

Despite the above, there are some fundamental drawbacks along with blockchain deployment. The motivation behind blockchains is to minimize trust for data transitions. Nevertheless, when blockchains track real-world assets or facts, some trust must be indispensably present among participants. These participants include data suppliers, power-holding authorities, software vendors, and so on. Some adhoc remedies, such as legislation or reward mechanisms, are suggested along the way. The panacea, oracle services, are recently developed at a fast pace. They attempt to link the on-chain contracts with trusted off-chain facts [2]. Another hindrance to the wider blockchain adoption stems from the platform's inherent scalability, security, or utility problems. These are exemplified by the occasional jam of the Ethereum network and hacking accidents in cryptocurrency exchanges.

Let us go back to the fundamental question: when to use blockchains? In Chap. 2, we generally remark that the employment of blockchains for security reasons and databases for performance in data processing. After examining the above use cases, we can now narrow down the blockchain applicability as opposed to other security solutions. In essence, blockchains *disintermediate*. Practically, mutually distrusting parties can pre-agree on an anti-dispute rule and encode the state transition as a smart contract. The decentralized architecture allows contracts to fairly execute as intended without interference from any single party. In the above use cases, disputes can be on ownership of assets, records, and identities. In the case of Automatic Money Makers, the state transition pertains to swap tokens at a transparent rate. Besides, we agree with some applications that use a global permissionless blockchain as a repository with universal accessibility. Users can leverage its highly available, verifiable service without maintenance costs. Clear to see, financial sectors and identity management call for more openness and transparency. Permissionless blockchains are more appropriate for them. In contrast, memberships are fixed in supply chain and healthcare sectors. These industries come with a strong demand on data privacy. Hence, permissioned blockchains will be a better choice to resolve the conflicts among parties in such sectors.

Yet, we have also seen some worrying trends in the distorted usage of blockchains. Particularly, these applications operate in a closed-membership setting. They do not require the openness and transparency delivered by permissionless blockchains. But they completely ignore the disintermediation nature of blockchains. Instead, they attempt to only use it as a tamper-evident storage. They even deploy suppose-to-be-decentralized blockchain nodes in a single administered domain. In other words, there exists a single entity to manage the nodes and the network. From our understanding, blockchains for them are definitely an overkill. (In our perspective, it is as silly as driving an airplane with its landing gear like a car.) We strongly advise against blockchain usage of this sort. Instead, a secure database could be a better alternative [93, 275, 296]. Like blockchains, secure databases also provide verifiable data storage. However, unlike blockchains, they are centralized and do not disintermediate. Nor can they settle disputes without a single-point interference—administrators are technically capable to hamper execution or tamper records, whereas secure databases are only capable to learn their action trails. As far as we are concerned with these closed-membership applications only calling for access verifiability, the centralization in secure databases is worthwhile for the sake of high performance.

Again, to appeal to interested readers, we compile related surveys in Table 4.1. Surveys and individual papers flesh out more details on their blockchain usages. As we can see, blockchains and their applications have pervaded all aspects of life. With the proliferation of blockchains and decentralization, some experts picture a new era called Web 3.0 [75]. While the first and second eras of the Web both hinge the centralized Internet vendors, Web 3.0 envisions a new era of the World Wide Web with no monopolies and trusted intermediaries, all credited to the blockchain technology as the cornerstone. Ideally, for each activity in real

Table 4.1 Blockchain application surveys

Domain	References
Finance	[124, 281, 295, 295]
Supply Chain	[82, 163, 179, 250]
Healthcare	[86, 208, 210, 297]
Identity Management	[97, 141, 171, 192]

life, we can find a decentralized counterpart in Web 3.0. For example, monetary transfers are powered by cryptocurrency rather than the conventional banking systems, proof-of-ownerships via NFT instead of custodial authorities, trading via Decentralized Financial (DeFi) instruments as opposed to central exchanges, and collective decision-making by Decentralized Autonomous Organizations (DAO) [19] rather than electoral politics. Despite this, Web 3.0 is not born without skeptics. Not mentioning the technical difficulties, poor accessibility, rampant speculations, and out-of-place regulations are all serious hurdles for the advancement of Web 3.0. Bearing the hallmark of decentralization, will Web 3.0 spring up against all odds, like the previous two? Or it will gradually fizzle out into obscurity? We believe it all comes down to a more fundamental problem—are the public more favorable to decentralization and its accompanying properties like freedom or censorship-resistance? Perhaps they would prefer centralization with its efficiency and governance. Let us end the book with this philosophical question and leave it for the readers to answer.

Acknowledgements We would like to thank various colleagues for their help and suggestions. In particular, we would like to thank Prof. Beng Chin Ooi for getting us to start the writing of this book and his help in proofreading and editing. We would like to thank the NUS School of Computing DBSystems, FabricSharp, and BlockBench colleagues for their contributions and discussions.
Pingcheng Ruan and Dumitrel Loghin's work is supported by Singapore Blockchain Innovation Programme (SBIP). This project is supported by the National Research Foundation, Singapore, under its Emerging Areas Research Projects (EARP) Funding Initiative. Any opinions, findings, conclusions, or recommendations expressed in this material are those of the author(s) and do not reflect the views of the National Research Foundation, Singapore.
Tien Tuan Anh Dinh's work is supported by the Singapore University of Technology and Design's start-up grant SRG-ISTD-2019-144. Meihui Zhang's work is supported by the National Natural Science Foundation of China (62072033) and CCF-AFSG Research Fund (RF20200015).

Appendix

A

A.1 Basic Cryptographic Primitives

- **Hash Functions** ($y = Hash(x)$) are a class of functions that map an input x of arbitrary size to an output y of fixed size. These functions have the following properties: pre-image resistance and collision resistance. The first property, namely pre-image resistance, means that it is computationally infeasible to reverse the function, i.e., recovering the input x for an output y such that $y = Hash(x)$. Collision resistance implies it is computationally infeasible to find two inputs sharing the same output, i.e., finding any pair of $x1$ and $x2$ such that $Hash(x1) = Hash(x2)$. Popular implementations of hash functions include but are not limited to MD5 and SHA256. Hash functions are widely used in blockchains and other applications for data integrity.
- **Asymmetric Cryptography** is a message encryption technique that uses a pair of related keys, a public key and a private key. The public key pk is known by senders to encrypt the message m, such that the enciphered text is $e = encrypt(m, pk)$. The private key sk is held confidentially by recipients, and it is used for deciphering m, such as $m = decrypt(e, sk)$. Beyond encryption, asymmetric cryptography can be used for digital signature, where the roles of the two keys are reversed. The private key holder encrypts the data with its private key, amounting to signing. The encrypted data are decrypted by holders of the public key, amounting to verification. If successful, the message sender is authenticated to be the private key holder. Asymmetric cryptography is used in blockchains to verify the identity of transaction issuers and attest to the exclusive ownership of cryptocurrencies.
- **Merkle Tree** [209] is a special form of a binary tree where tree leaves represent data hashes and tree node pointers are implemented as hashes referencing child nodes. By the recursive nature of trees and cryptographic properties of hash functions, the Merkle tree root can uniquely identify the underlying content. The querying path from the root

P. Ruan et al., *Blockchains*, Synthesis Lectures on Data Management, https://doi.org/10.1007/978-3-031-13979-6

node to a data node can serve as an integrity proof. Merkle trees are extensively used in blockchains for ensuring data integrity.

- **Verifiable Random Function** is an asymmetric-key version of a cryptographic hash [71]. It also transforms an input x into a fixed-length value y, which sheds little hints on x. In addition, a VRF value y is dependent on a peer's private key sk. VRF outputs a proof π to attest the correspondence from x and sk to y. Provided with the public key pk, the correspondence can be easily verified as a hash function.

A.2   Gallery of Popular Blockchains

- **Bitcoin** [220] is the first-ever practical peer-to-peer cryptocurrency system. Designed by a hacker with the pseudonym Satoshi Nakamoto, Bitcoin introduces the concept of blockchain and ingeniously employs Proof-of-Work to address Byzantine-fault tolerance in a permissionless setting.
- **Litecoin** [40] is a fork of Bitcoin and inherits most of its features, except for some adjusted parameters. Litecoin's block interval is reduced from 10 min to 2.5 min. The total cryptocurrency supply is enlarged to 84 million as opposed to 21 million in Bitcoin.
- **Ethereum** [282] is the first-ever programmable permissionless blockchain. It first ushers in the concept of smart contracts, so that users can encode arbitrary data transitions on blockchain by sending transactions to invoke these smart contracts.
- **Solana** [287] is a permissionless blockchain that was born to rival Ethereum. It uniquely utilizes Proof-of-History to achieve Byzantine consensus. Its native token is SOL and it supports smart contracts to customize the transaction validation.
- **Quorum** [53] is the permissioned version of Ethereum. It inherits most features of Ethereum, except that it replaces the Proof-of-Work consensus with state-machine replication. Quorum targets business users and it is designed with confidentially support, achieved by its private transactions.
- **R3 Corda** [217] is a permissioned blockchain designed for the financial sector. It is built with a number of native operations, specially tailored for financial usages, such as asset management and business logic automation.
- **Hyperledger Fabric** [91] is a permissioned blockchain initially developed by IBM, with an eye on business usage. Fabric has a distinctive execute-order-validate transaction pipeline, where transactions are firstly simulated and then sequenced into the ledger.
- **Diem** [61] is a permissioned blockchain developed by Facebook aiming to create a global-accessible financial infrastructure. It uses HotStuff [289] as its Byzantine-fault tolerance core and it supports smart contracts.

- **Ripple** [94] is a permissioned blockchain with an aim to facilitate global cross-border payment, akin to building a decentralized Swift-like system. XRP is its native token. Ripple's consensus is achieved by transaction validation by a committee of bank-owned servers.

Bibliography

1. A Comprehensive List of Cryptocurrency Exchange Hacks. https://selfkey.org/list-of-cryptocurrency-exchange-hacks/.
2. A Guide To the Top 5 Decentralized Oracle Projects in Crypto. https://cryptoticker.io/en/top-5-crypto-oracles/.
3. Aave. https://aave.com/.
4. Amazon Dynamodb. https://aws.amazon.com/dynamodb.
5. Amazon Quantum Ledger Database (Qldb). https://aws.amazon.com/qldb/.
6. Atomic Swap. https://en.bitcoin.it/wiki/Atomic_swap.
7. Banksy Art Burned Destroyed and Sold as Token in 'Money-Making Stunt'. https://www.bbc.com/news/technology-56335948.
8. Bitcoin Cash. https://en.wikipedia.org/wiki/Bitcoin_Cash.
9. Blockchain Interoperability : Why Is Cross Chain Technology Important? https://101blockchains.com/blockchain-interoperability/.
10. Caliper. https://hyperledger.github.io/caliper/.
11. Cassandra. https://techcommunity.microsoft.com/t5/sql-server/serializable-vs-snapshot-isolation-level/ba-p/383281.
12. Cassandra. https://cassandra.apache.org/.
13. Cockroachdb. https://github.com/cockroachdb/cockroach.
14. Compound. https://compound.finance/.
15. Constructor Modifier. https://github.com/ethereum/solidity/issues/3196.
16. Cosmos Ibc: Inter-Blockchain Communication Protocol. https://docs.cosmos.network/master/ibc/overview.html#.
17. Cve-2018-10299. https://nvd.nist.gov/vuln/detail/CVE-2018-10299.
18. Dai. https://makerdao.com/en/.
19. Decentralized Autonomous Organization (DAO). https://www.investopedia.com/tech/what-dao/.
20. Deversifi: Layer 2 Exchange Guide. https://blog.deversifi.com/layer-2-exchange-guide/.
21. Discover: a Static Analyzer To Find Bugs in Computer Programs and Smart Contracts. https://www.comp.nus.edu.sg/~dbsystem/discover/.
22. Dpos. https://en.bitcoinwiki.org/wiki/DPoS.

© The Editor(s) (if applicable) and The Author(s), under exclusive license to Springer
Nature Switzerland AG 2022
P. Ruan et al., *Blockchains*, Synthesis Lectures on Data Management,
https://doi.org/10.1007/978-3-031-13979-6

23. Dydx: Perpetuals Decentralized. https://dydx.exchange/.
24. Ens: Decentralised Naming for Wallets Websites & More. https://ens.domains/.
25. Eosio. https://eos.io/.
26. Erc-20 Token Standard. https://ethereum.org/en/developers/docs/standards/tokens/erc-20/.
27. Erc-721 Token Standard. https://ethereum.org/en/developers/docs/standards/tokens/erc-721/.
28. Etcd: Distributed Reliable Key-Value Store for the Most Critical Data of a Distributed System. https://github.com/etcd-io/etcd.
29. Ethereum. https://ethereum.org/.
30. Ethereum 2.0 (Eth2). https://ethereum.org/en/eth2/.
31. Ethereum Oracles. https://ethereum.org/en/developers/docs/oracles/.
32. Ethereum Smart Contract Best Practices. https://consensys.github.io/smart-contract-best-practices/recommendations/.
33. Ethereum Unleashed the "Initial Coin Offering" Craze But It Can'T Handle Its Insane Success. https://qz.com/1004892/the-bancor-ico-just-raised-153-million-on-ethereum-in-three-hours/.
34. Fabric V0.6. https://hyperledger-fabric.readthedocs.io/en/v0.6/home.html.
35. Fisco-bcos. https://http://fisco-bcos.org//.
36. HammerDB. https://www.hammerdb.com/.
37. Hyperledger Fabric. https://www.hyperledger.org/use/fabric.
38. Ico. https://en.wikipedia.org/wiki/Initial_coin_offering.
39. Kafka. https://kafka.apache.org/.
40. Litecoin. https://litecoin.com/.
41. Medilot. https://medilot.com/.
42. Merkle Patricia Tree. https://github.com/ethereum/wiki/wiki/Patricia-Tree.
43. Mongodb. https://www.mongodb.com.
44. Multichain. https://www.multichain.com/.
45. Nash. https://nash.io/.
46. Optimistic   Rollups.   https://docs.ethhub.io/ethereum-roadmap/layer-2-scaling/optimistic_rollups/.
47. Parity. https://www.parity.io/.
48. Payment Channels. https://en.bitcoin.it/wiki/Payment_channels.
49. Polkadot's Cross-Chain Message-Passing Protocol. https://research.web3.foundation/en/latest/polkadot/XCMP/index.html.
50. Predicting Random Numbers in Ethereum Smart Contracts. https://blog.positive.com/predicting-random-numbers-in-ethereum-smart-contracts-e5358c6b8620.
51. Proof of Stake. https://en.wikipedia.org/wiki/Proof_of_stake.
52. Provenance. https://www.provenance.org/whitepaper.
53. Quorum. https://consensys.net/quorum/.
54. R3 Corda. https://www.corda.net/.
55. Rubixi Contract. https://etherscan.io/address/0xe82719202e5965Cf5D9B6673B7503a3b92DE20be#contracts.
56. Spanner. https://cloud.google.com/spanner.
57. Starkware. https://starkware.co/.
58. Sushiswap. https://sushi.com/.
59. Sysbench. https://github.com/akopytov/sysbench.
60. Tether. https://tether.to/.
61. The Diem Blockchain. https://developers.diem.com/docs/technical-papers/the-diem-blockchain-paper/.

62. The Ethereum Network Is Getting Jammed Up Because People Are Rushing To Buy Cartoon Cats on Its Blockchain. https://qz.com/1145833/cryptokitties-is-causing-ethereum-network-congestion/.

63. The Everledger Platform. https://everledger.io/.

64. Tidb. https://github.com/pingcap/tidb.

65. Tidb-bench: TiDB standard test suite. https://github.com/pingcap/tidb-bench.

66. Tomodex. https://dex.tomochain.com/home/.

67. Top 10 Blockchain Security and Smart Contract Audit Companies. https://boxmining.com/top-blockchain-security-firms/.

68. TPC-C: an On-Line Transaction Processing Benchmark . https://www.tpc.org/tpcc/.

69. Trusted Execution Environment. https://en.wikipedia.org/wiki/Trusted_execution_environment.

70. Uniswap. https://uniswap.org/.

71. Verifiable Random Function. https://en.wikipedia.org/wiki/Verifiable_random_function.

72. Verifiable Secret Sharing. https://en.wikipedia.org/wiki/Verifiable_secret_sharing.

73. Verisign Issues False Microsoft Digital Certificates. https://www.computerworld.com/article/2798454/verisign-issues-false-microsoft-digital-certificates.html.

74. Vyper: a Contract-Oriented Pythonic Programming Language That Targets the Ethereum Virtual Machine (Evm). https://github.com/vyperlang/vyper.

75. Web 3.0. https://en.wikipedia.org/wiki/Web3.

76. What Is Miner Extractable Value (Mev)? https://coinmarketcap.com/alexandria/glossary/miner-extractable-value-mev.

77. Why Sharding Is Great: Demystifying the Technical Properties. https://vitalik.ca/general/2021/04/07/sharding.html.

78. Zk-rollups. https://docs.ethhub.io/ethereum-roadmap/layer-2-scaling/zk-rollups/.

79. "performance Benchmarking Results for Corda". https://docs.corda.net/docs/corda-enterprise/4.5/node/performance-results.html, 2020. [Online; accessed 01-September-2020].

80. How Fast Is Redis?, 2021.

81. Tidb Sysbench Performance Test Report – V4.0 Vs. V3.0, 2021.

82. S. A. Abeyratne and R. P. Monfared. Blockchain Ready Manufacturing Supply Chain Using Distributed Ledger. *International Journal of Research in Engineering and Technology*, 5(9):1–10, 2016.

83. I. Abraham, G. Gueta, D. Malkhi, L. Alvisi, R. Kotla, and J.-P. Martin. Revisiting Fast Practical Byzantine Fault Tolerance. *arXiv preprint* arXiv:1712.01367, 2017.

84. I. Abraham, D. Malkhi, K. Nayak, and L. Ren. Dfinity Consensus Explored. *IACR Cryptol. ePrint Arch.*, 2018:1153, 2018.

85. I. Abraham, D. Malkhi, K. Nayak, L. Ren, and M. Yin. Sync Hotstuff: Simple and Practical Synchronous State Machine Replication. In *2020 IEEE Symposium on Security and Privacy (SP)*, pages 106–118. IEEE, 2020.

86. C. C. Agbo, Q. H. Mahmoud, and J. M. Eklund. Blockchain Technology in Healthcare: a Systematic Review. In *Healthcare*, volume 7, page 56. Multidisciplinary Digital Publishing Institute, 2019.

87. M. Al-Bassam, A. Sonnino, S. Bano, D. Hrycyszyn, and G. Danezis. Chainspace: a Sharded Smart Contracts Platform. *arXiv preprint* arXiv:1708.03778, 2017.

88. L. Allen, P. Antonopoulos, A. Arasu, J. Gehrke, J. Hammer, J. Hunter, R. Kaushik, D. Kossmann, J. Lee, R. Ramamurthy, S. Setty, J. Szymaszek, A. van Renen, and R. Venkatesan. Veritas: Shared Verifiable Databases and Tables in the Cloud. In *CIDR*, 2019.

89. M. J. Amiri, D. Agrawal, and A. El Abbadi. Parblockchain: Leveraging Transaction Parallelism in Permissioned Blockchain Systems. In *2019 IEEE 39th International Conference on Distributed Computing Systems (ICDCS)*, pages 1337–1347. IEEE, 2019.

90. J. C. Anderson, J. Lehnardt, and N. Slater. *Couchdb: the Definitive Guide: Time To Relax.* "O'Reilly Media, Inc.", 2010.

91. E. Androulaki, A. Barger, V. Bortnikov, C. Cachin, K. Christidis, A. De Caro, D. Enyeart, C. Ferris, G. Laventman, Y. Manevich, et al. Hyperledger Fabric: a Distributed Operating System for Permissioned Blockchains. In *Proceedings of the thirteenth EuroSys conference*, pages 1–15, 2018.

92. M. Apostolaki, A. Zohar, and L. Vanbever. Hijacking bitcoin: Routing attacks on cryptocurrencies. In *2017 IEEE symposium on security and privacy (SP)*, pages 375–392. IEEE, 2017.

93. A. Arasu, K. Eguro, R. Kaushik, D. Kossmann, P. Meng, V. Pandey, and R. Ramamurthy. Concerto: a High Concurrency Key-Value Store With Integrity. In *Proceedings of the 2017 ACM International Conference on Management of Data*, pages 251–266, 2017.

94. F. Armknecht, G. O. Karame, A. Mandal, F. Youssef, and E. Zenner. Ripple: Overview and outlook. In *International conference on trust and trustworthy computing*, pages 163–180. Springer, 2015.

95. N. Atzei, M. Bartoletti, and T. Cimoli. A Survey of Attacks on Ethereum Smart Contracts (Sok). In *International conference on principles of security and trust*, pages 164–186. Springer, 2017.

96. G. Avarikioti, E. Kokoris-Kogias, and R. Wattenhofer. Divide and Scale: Formalization of Distributed Ledger Sharding Protocols. *arXiv preprint* arXiv:1910.10434, 2019.

97. D. Baars. Towards Self-Sovereign Identity Using Blockchain Technology. Master's thesis, University of Twente, 2016.

98. A. Back, M. Corallo, L. Dashjr, M. Friedenbach, G. Maxwell, A. Miller, A. Poelstra, J. Timón, and P. Wuille. Enabling Blockchain Innovations With Pegged Sidechains. *URL:* http://www.opensciencereview.com/papers/123/enablingblockchain-innovations-with-pegged-sidechains, 72, 2014.

99. P. Bailis, A. Davidson, A. Fekete, A. Ghodsi, J. M. Hellerstein, and I. Stoica. Highly Available Transactions: Virtues and Limitations. *PVLDB*, 7(3):181–192, 2013.

100. M. Balakrishnan, D. Malkhi, V. Prabhakaran, T. Wobber, M. Wei, and J. D. Davis. Corfu: a Shared Log Design for Flash Clusters. In *Proc. of 9th USENIX Conference on Networked Systems Design and Implementation*, 2012.

101. M. Balakrishnan, D. Malkhi, T. Wobber, M. Wu, V. Prabhakaran, M. Wei, J. D. Davis, S. Rao, T. Zou, and A. Zuck. Tango: Distributed Data Structures Over a Shared Log. In *Proc. of 24th ACM Symposium on Operating Systems Principles*, pages 325–340, 2013.

102. A. Baliga, I. Subhod, P. Kamat, and S. Chatterjee. Performance Evaluation of the Quorum Blockchain Platform. *arXiv preprint* arXiv:1809.03421, 2018.

103. S. Bano, A. Sonnino, M. Al-Bassam, S. Azouvi, P. McCorry, S. Meiklejohn, and G. Danezis. Sok: Consensus in the Age of Blockchains. In *Proceedings of the 1st ACM Conference on Advances in Financial Technologies*, pages 183–198, 2019.

104. J. Beccuti, C. Jaag, et al. The Bitcoin Mining Game: on the Optimality of Honesty in Proof-Of-Work Consensus Mechanism. *Swiss Economics Working Paper 0060*, 2017.

105. R. Belchior, A. Vasconcelos, S. Guerreiro, and M. Correia. A Survey on Blockchain Interoperability: Past Present and Future Trends. *ACM Computing Surveys (CSUR)*, 54(8):1–41, 2021.

106. P. A. Bernstein, C. W. Reid, and S. Das. Hyder - a Transactional Record Manager for Shared Flash. In *CIDR*, 2011.

107. A. Bessani, J. Sousa, and E. E. Alchieri. State Machine Replication for the Masses With Bft-Smart. In *2014 44th Annual IEEE/IFIP International Conference on Dependable Systems and Networks*, pages 355–362. IEEE, 2014.

108. J. Bonneau, A. Miller, J. Clark, A. Narayanan, J. A. Kroll, and E. W. Felten. Sok: Research Perspectives and Challenges for Bitcoin and Cryptocurrencies. In *2015 IEEE symposium on security and privacy*, pages 104–121. IEEE, 2015.

109. G. Bracha. Asynchronous Byzantine Agreement Protocols. *Information and Computation*, 75(2):130–143, 1987.

110. L. Breidenbach, C. Cachin, B. Chan, A. Coventry, S. Ellis, A. Juels, F. Koushanfar, A. Miller, B. Magauran, D. Moroz, et al. Chainlink 2.0: Next Steps in the Evolution of Decentralized Oracle Networks, 2021.

111. E. Buchman. *Tendermint: Byzantine Fault Tolerance in the Age of Blockchains*. PhD thesis, The University of Guelph, 2016.

112. N. Budhiraja, K. Marzullo, F. B. Schneider, and S. Toueg. The Primary-Backup Approach. *Distributed systems*, 2:199–216, 1993.

113. V. Buterin. An Incomplete Guide To Rollups, 2021.

114. M. J. Cahill, U. Röhm, and A. D. Fekete. Serializable isolation for snapshot databases. *ACM Transactions on Database Systems (TODS)*, 34(4):1–42, 2009.

115. J. L. Carlson. *Redis in Action*. Manning Shelter Island, 2013.

116. M. Carlsten. *The Impact of Transaction Fees on Bitcoin Mining Strategies*. PhD thesis, Princeton University, 2016.

117. V. H. Castillo, A. I. Martínez-García, and J. Pulido. A Knowledge-Based Taxonomy of Critical Factors for Adopting Electronic Health Record Systems by Physicians: a Systematic Literature Review. *BMC medical informatics and decision making*, 10(1):1–17, 2010.

118. M. Castro, B. Liskov, et al. Practical Byzantine Fault Tolerance. In *OSDI*, volume 99, pages 173–186, 1999.

119. J. A. Chacko, R. Mayer, and H.-A. Jacobsen. Why Do My Blockchain Transactions Fail? a Study of Hyperledger Fabric. In *Proceedings of the 2021 International Conference on Management of Data*, pages 221–234, 2021.

120. H. Chen, M. Pendleton, L. Njilla, and S. Xu. A Survey on Ethereum Systems Security: Vulnerabilities Attacks and Defenses. *ACM Computing Surveys (CSUR)*, 53(3):1–43, 2020.

121. S. Chen, J. Zhang, R. Shi, J. Yan, and Q. Ke. A Comparative Testing on Performance of Blockchain and Relational Database: Foundation for Applying Smart Technology Into Current Business Systems. In *International Conference on Distributed, Ambient, and Pervasive Interactions*, pages 21–34. Springer, 2018.

122. T. Chen, Z. Li, Y. Zhu, J. Chen, X. Luo, J. C.-S. Lui, X. Lin, and X. Zhang. Understanding Ethereum Via Graph Analysis. *ACM Transactions on Internet Technology (TOIT)*, 20(2):1–32, 2020.

123. W. Chen, T. Zhang, Z. Chen, Z. Zheng, and Y. Lu. Traveling the Token World: a Graph Analysis of Ethereum Erc20 Token Ecosystem. In *Proceedings of The Web Conference 2020*, pages 1411–1421, 2020.

124. Y. Chen and C. Bellavitis. Blockchain Disruption and Decentralized Finance: the Rise of Decentralized Business Models. *Journal of Business Venturing Insights*, 13:e00151, 2020.

125. M. J. M. Chowdhury, A. Colman, M. A. Kabir, J. Han, and P. Sarda. Blockchain Versus Database: a Critical Analysis. In *2018 17th IEEE International Conference On Trust, Security And Privacy In Computing And Communications/12th IEEE International Conference On Big Data Science And Engineering (TrustCom/BigDataSE)*, pages 1348–1353. IEEE, 2018.

126. M. Conti, E. S. Kumar, C. Lal, and S. Ruj. A Survey on Security and Privacy Issues of Bitcoin. *IEEE Communications Surveys & Tutorials*, 20(4):3416–3452, 2018.

127. B. F. Cooper, A. Silberstein, E. Tam, R. Ramakrishnan, and R. Sears. Benchmarking cloud serving systems with ycsb. In *Proceedings of the 1st ACM symposium on Cloud computing*, pages 143–154, 2010.

128. J. C. Corbett, J. Dean, M. Epstein, A. Fikes, C. Frost, J. J. Furman, S. Ghemawat, A. Gubarev, C. Heiser, P. Hochschild, et al. Spanner: Google'S Globally Distributed Database. *ACM Transactions on Computer Systems (TOCS)*, 31(3):1–22, 2013.

129. M. Crosby, P. Pattanayak, S. Verma, V. Kalyanaraman, et al. Blockchain Technology: Beyond Bitcoin. *Applied Innovation*, 2(6-10):71, 2016.

130. R. Dahlberg, T. Pulls, and R. Peeters. Efficient Sparse Merkle Trees: Caching Strategies and Secure (Non-)Membership Proofs. Cryptology ePrint Archive, Report 2016/683, 2016.

131. P. Daian, S. Goldfeder, T. Kell, Y. Li, X. Zhao, I. Bentov, L. Breidenbach, and A. Juels. Flash Boys 2.0: Frontrunning in Decentralized Exchanges Miner Extractable Value and Consensus Instability. In *2020 IEEE Symposium on Security and Privacy (SP)*, pages 910–927. IEEE, 2020.

132. G. Danezis and S. Meiklejohn. Centrally Banked Cryptocurrencies. *arXiv preprint* arXiv:1505.06895, 2015.

133. H. Dang, T. T. A. Dinh, D. Loghin, E.-C. Chang, Q. Lin, and B. C. Ooi. Towards Scaling Blockchain Systems Via Sharding. In *Proceedings of the 2019 international conference on management of data*, pages 123–140, 2019.

134. T. Dickerson, P. Gazzillo, M. Herlihy, and E. Koskinen. Adding Concurrency To Smart Contracts. *Distributed Computing*, 33(3):209–225, 2020.

135. D. E. Difallah, A. Pavlo, C. Curino, and P. Cudre-Mauroux. Oltp-bench: An extensible testbed for benchmarking relational databases. *Proceedings of the VLDB Endowment*, 7(4):277–288, 2013.

136. T. T. A. Dinh, A. Datta, and B. C. Ooi. A Blueprint for Interoperable Blockchains. *arXiv preprint* arXiv:1910.00985, 2019.

137. T. T. A. Dinh, R. Liu, M. Zhang, G. Chen, B. C. Ooi, and J. Wang. Untangling Blockchain: a Data Processing View of Blockchain Systems. *IEEE transactions on knowledge and data engineering*, 30(7):1366–1385, 2018.

138. T. T. A. Dinh, J. Wang, G. Chen, R. Liu, B. C. Ooi, and K.-L. Tan. Blockbench: a Framework for Analyzing Private Blockchains. In *Proc. of ACM International Conference on Management of Data*, pages 1085–1100. ACM, 2017.

139. M. Dotan, Y.-A. Pignolet, S. Schmid, S. Tochner, and A. Zohar. Cryptocurrency Networking: Context State-Of-The-Art Challenges. 2020.

140. S. Duan, M. K. Reiter, and H. Zhang. Beat: Asynchronous Bft Made Practical. In *Proceedings of the 2018 ACM SIGSAC Conference on Computer and Communications Security*, pages 2028–2041, 2018.

141. P. Dunphy and F. A. Petitcolas. A First Look At Identity Management Schemes on the Blockchain. *IEEE security & privacy*, 16(4):20–29, 2018.

142. M. El-Hindi, C. Binnig, A. Arasu, D. Kossmann, and R. Ramamurthy. Blockchaindb: a Shared Database on Blockchains. *PVLDB*, 12(11):1597–1609, 2019.

143. etcd. Understanding Performance. https://bit.ly/2kzI8R2, 2019.

144. I. Eyal. The Miner'S Dilemma. In *2015 IEEE Symposium on Security and Privacy*, pages 89–103. IEEE, 2015.

145. I. Eyal, A. E. Gencer, E. G. Sirer, and R. Van Renesse. Bitcoin-ng: a Scalable Blockchain Protocol. In *13th {USENIX} symposium on networked systems design and implementation ({NSDI} 16)*, pages 45–59, 2016.

146. I. Eyal and E. G. Sirer. Majority Is Not Enough: Bitcoin Mining Is Vulnerable. In *International conference on financial cryptography and data security*, pages 436–454. Springer, 2014.

147. C. Feng and J. Niu. Selfish Mining in Ethereum. In *2019 IEEE 39th International Conference on Distributed Computing Systems (ICDCS)*, pages 1306–1316. IEEE, 2019.

148. M. J. Fischer, N. A. Lynch, and M. S. Paterson. Impossibility of Distributed Consensus With One Faulty Process. *Journal of the ACM (JACM)*, 32(2):374–382, 1985.
149. A. Gaihre, Y. Luo, and H. Liu. Do Bitcoin Users Really Care About Anonymity? An Analysis of the Bitcoin Transaction Graph. In *2018 IEEE International Conference on Big Data (Big Data)*, pages 1198–1207. IEEE, 2018.
150. J. Garay, A. Kiayias, and N. Leonardos. The Bitcoin Backbone Protocol: Analysis and Applications. In *Annual international conference on the theory and applications of cryptographic techniques*, pages 281–310. Springer, 2015.
151. Z. Ge, D. Loghin, B. C. Ooi, P. Ruan, and T. Wang. Hybrid Blockchain Database Systems: Design and Performance. *VLDB Endowment*, 15(5):1092 – 1104, 2022.
152. A. Gervais, G. O. Karame, K. Wust, V. Glykantzis, H. Ritzdorf, and S. Capkun. On the Security and Performance of Proof of Work Blockchains. In *Proceedings of the 2016 ACM SIGSAC conference on computer and communications security*, pages 3–16, 2016.
153. Y. Gilad, R. Hemo, S. Micali, G. Vlachos, and N. Zeldovich. Algorand: Scaling Byzantine Agreements for Cryptocurrencies. In *Proceedings of the 26th symposium on operating systems principles*, pages 51–68, 2017.
154. S. Gilbert and N. Lynch. Perspectives on the Cap Theorem. *Computer*, 45(2):30–36, 2012.
155. J. Göbel, H. P. Keeler, A. E. Krzesinski, and P. G. Taylor. Bitcoin Blockchain Dynamics: the Selfish-Mine Strategy in the Presence of Propagation Delay. *Performance Evaluation*, 104:23–41, 2016.
156. C. Gorenflo, L. Golab, and S. Keshav. Xox Fabric: a Hybrid Approach To Blockchain Transaction Execution. In *2020 IEEE International Conference on Blockchain and Cryptocurrency (ICBC)*, pages 1–9. IEEE, 2020.
157. L. Gudgeon, P. Moreno-Sanchez, S. Roos, P. McCorry, and A. Gervais. Sok: Off the Chain Transactions. *IACR Cryptol. ePrint Arch.*, 2019:360, 2019.
158. L. Gudgeon, P. Moreno-Sanchez, S. Roos, P. McCorry, and A. Gervais. Sok: Layer-Two Blockchain Protocols. In *International Conference on Financial Cryptography and Data Security*, pages 201–226. Springer, 2020.
159. G. G. Gueta, I. Abraham, S. Grossman, D. Malkhi, B. Pinkas, M. Reiter, D.-A. Seredinschi, O. Tamir, and A. Tomescu. Sbft: a Scalable and Decentralized Trust Infrastructure. In *2019 49th Annual IEEE/IFIP international conference on dependable systems and networks (DSN)*, pages 568–580. IEEE, 2019.
160. B. Guo, Z. Lu, Q. Tang, J. Xu, and Z. Zhang. Dumbo: Faster Asynchronous Bft Protocols. In *Proceedings of the 2020 ACM SIGSAC Conference on Computer and Communications Security*, pages 803–818, 2020.
161. D. Guo, J. Dong, and K. Wang. Graph Structure and Statistical Properties of Ethereum Transaction Relationships. *Information Sciences*, 492:58–71, 2019.
162. S. Gupta, S. Rahnama, J. Hellings, and M. Sadoghi. Resilientdb: Global Scale Resilient Blockchain Fabric. *arXiv preprint* arXiv:2002.00160, 2020.
163. N. Hackius and M. Petersen. Blockchain in Logistics and Supply Chain: Trick or Treat? In *Digitalization in Supply Chain Management and Logistics: Smart and Digital Solutions for an Industry 4.0 Environment. Proceedings of the Hamburg International Conference of Logistics (HICL), Vol. 23*, pages 3–18. Berlin: epubli GmbH, 2017.
164. E. Heilman, A. Kendler, A. Zohar, and S. Goldberg. Eclipse attacks on bitcoin's peer-to-peer network. In *24th USENIX Security Symposium (USENIX Security 15)*, pages 129–144, 2015.
165. J. Hellings and M. Sadoghi. Brief Announcement: the Fault-Tolerant Cluster-Sending Problem. In *33rd International Symposium on Distributed Computing (DISC 2019)*. Schloss Dagstuhl-Leibniz-Zentrum fuer Informatik, 2019.

166. M. Herlihy. Atomic Cross-Chain Swaps. In *Proceedings of the 2018 ACM symposium on principles of distributed computing*, pages 245–254, 2018.

167. M. Herlihy, B. Liskov, and L. Shrira. Cross-chain Deals and Adversarial Commerce. *The VLDB Journal*, pages 1–19, 2021.

168. Y. Huang, J. Tang, Q. Cong, A. Lim, and J. Xu. Do the Rich Get Richer? Fairness Analysis for Blockchain Incentives. In *Proceedings of the 2021 International Conference on Management of Data*, pages 790–803, 2021.

169. V. Ihnatiuk. Tendermint Review . http://archive.today/fU9wO, 2022.

170. Z. István, A. Sorniotti, and M. Vukolić. Streamchain: Do Blockchains Need Blocks? In *Proceedings of the 2nd Workshop on Scalable and Resilient Infrastructures for Distributed Ledgers*, pages 1–6, 2018.

171. O. Jacobovitz. Blockchain for Identity Management. *The Lynne and William Frankel Center for Computer Science Department of Computer Science. Ben-Gurion University, Beer Sheva*, 2016.

172. R. Kallman, H. Kimura, J. Natkins, A. Pavlo, A. Rasin, S. Zdonik, E. P. Jones, S. Madden, M. Stonebraker, Y. Zhang, et al. H-store: a High-Performance Distributed Main Memory Transaction Processing System. *Proc. of VLDB Endowment*, 1(2):1496–1499, 2008.

173. A. Kiayias and G. Panagiotakos. Speed-security Tradeoffs in Blockchain Protocols. *IACR Cryptol. ePrint Arch.*, 2015:1019, 2015.

174. L. Kiffer, R. Rajaraman, and A. Shelat. A Better Method To Analyze Blockchain Consistency. In *Proceedings of the 2018 ACM SIGSAC Conference on Computer and Communications Security*, pages 729–744, 2018.

175. C. Kim, J. Chhugani, N. Satish, E. Sedlar, A. D. Nguyen, T. Kaldewey, V. W. Lee, S. A. Brandt, and P. Dubey. Fast: Fast Architecture Sensitive Tree Search on Modern Cpus and Gpus. In *Proc. of ACM SIGMOD International Conference on Management of Data*, pages 339–350. ACM, 2010.

176. S. King. Primecoin: Cryptocurrency With Prime Number Proof-Of-Work. *July 7th*, 1(6), 2013.

177. E. K. Kogias, P. Jovanovic, N. Gailly, I. Khoffi, L. Gasser, and B. Ford. Enhancing Bitcoin Security and Performance With Strong Consistency Via Collective Signing. In *25th usenix security symposium (usenix security 16)*, pages 279–296, 2016.

178. E. Kokoris-Kogias, P. Jovanovic, L. Gasser, N. Gailly, E. Syta, and B. Ford. Omniledger: a Secure Scale-Out Decentralized Ledger Via Sharding. In *2018 IEEE Symposium on Security and Privacy (SP)*, pages 583–598. IEEE, 2018.

179. K. Korpela, J. Hallikas, and T. Dahlberg. Digital Supply Chain Transformation Toward Blockchain Integration. In *proceedings of the 50th Hawaii international conference on system sciences*, 2017.

180. R. Kothari, B. Jakheliya, and V. Sawant. A Distributed Peer-To-Peer Storage Network. In *2019 International Conference on Smart Systems and Inventive Technology (ICSSIT)*, pages 576–582. IEEE, 2019.

181. R. Kotla, L. Alvisi, M. Dahlin, A. Clement, and E. Wong. Zyzzyva: Speculative Byzantine Fault Tolerance. In *Proceedings of twenty-first ACM SIGOPS symposium on Operating systems principles*, pages 45–58, 2007.

182. J. Krupp and C. Rossow. Teether: Gnawing At Ethereum To Automatically Exploit Smart Contracts. In *27th {USENIX} Security Symposium ({USENIX} Security 18)*, pages 1317–1333, 2018.

183. J. Kuszmaul. Verkle Trees. *Verkle Trees*, pages 1–12, 2019.

184. P. Lafourcade and M. Lombard-Platet. About Blockchain Interoperability. *Information Processing Letters*, 161:105976, 2020.

185. A. Lakshman and P. Malik. Cassandra: a Decentralized Structured Storage System. *ACM SIGOPS Operating Systems Review*, 44(2):35–40, 2010.

186. L. Lamport. Generalized Consensus and Paxos. *Technical Report MSR-TR-2005-33, Microsoft Research*, 2005.

187. L. Lamport et al. Paxos Made Simple. *ACM Sigact News*, 32(4):18–25, 2001.

188. T. Leelavimolsilp, L. Tran-Thanh, and S. Stein. On the Preliminary Investigation of Selfish Mining Strategy With Multiple Selfish Miners. *arXiv preprint* arXiv:1802.02218, 2018.

189. C. Li, P. Li, D. Zhou, Z. Yang, M. Wu, G. Yang, W. Xu, F. Long, and A. C.-C. Yao. A Decentralized Blockchain With High Throughput and Fast Confirmation. In *2020 USENIX Annual Technical Conference (USENIX ATC 20)*, pages 515–528, 2020.

190. K. Li. The Blockchain Scalability Problem & the Race for Visa-Like Transaction Speed. http://archive.today/XnKJC, 2019.

191. X. Li, P. Jiang, T. Chen, X. Luo, and Q. Wen. A Survey on the Security of Blockchain Systems. *Future Generation Computer Systems*, 107:841–853, 2020.

192. S. Y. Lim, P. T. Fotsing, A. Almasri, O. Musa, M. L. M. Kiah, T. F. Ang, and R. Ismail. Blockchain Technology the Identity Management and Authentication Service Disruptor: a Survey. *International Journal on Advanced Science, Engineering and Information Technology*, 8(4-2):1735–1745, 2018.

193. I.-C. Lin and T.-C. Liao. A Survey of Blockchain Security Issues and Challenges. *Int. J. Netw. Secur.*, 19(5):653–659, 2017.

194. Q. Lin, K. Yang, T. T. A. Dinh, Q. Cai, G. Chen, B. C. Ooi, P. Ruan, S. Wang, Z. Xie, M. Zhang, et al. Forkbase: Immutable Tamper-Evident Storage Substrate for Branchable Applications. In *2020 IEEE 36th International Conference on Data Engineering (ICDE)*, pages 1718–1721. IEEE, 2020.

195. S. Liu, P. Viotti, C. Cachin, V. Quéma, and M. Vukolić. xft: Practical Fault Tolerance Beyond Crashes. In *12th {USENIX} Symposium on Operating Systems Design and Implementation ({OSDI} 16)*, pages 485–500, 2016.

196. X. F. Liu, X.-J. Jiang, S.-H. Liu, and C. K. Tse. Knowledge Discovery in Cryptocurrency Transactions: a Survey. *IEEE Access*, 9:37229–37254, 2021.

197. Y. Liu, J. Liu, M. A. V. Salles, Z. Zhang, T. Li, B. Hu, F. Henglein, and R. Lu. Building Blocks of Sharding Blockchain Systems: Concepts Approaches and Open Problems. *arXiv preprint* arXiv:2102.13364, 2021.

198. D. Loghin, G. Chen, T. T. A. Dinh, B. C. Ooi, and Y. M. Teo. Blockchain Goes Green? An Analysis of Blockchain on Low-Power Nodes. *arXiv preprint* arXiv:1905.06520, 2019.

199. D. Loghin, T. T. A. Dinh, A. Maw, C. Gang, Y. M. Teo, and B. C. Ooi. Blockchain Goes Green? Part II: Characterizing the Performance and Cost of Blockchains on the Cloud and at the Edge. *arXiv preprint* arXiv:2205.06941, 2022.

200. L. Luu, D.-H. Chu, H. Olickel, P. Saxena, and A. Hobor. Making Smart Contracts Smarter. In *Proceedings of the 2016 ACM SIGSAC conference on computer and communications security*, pages 254–269, 2016.

201. L. Luu, V. Narayanan, C. Zheng, K. Baweja, S. Gilbert, and P. Saxena. A Secure Sharding Protocol for Open Blockchains. In *Proceedings of the 2016 ACM SIGSAC Conference on Computer and Communications Security*, pages 17–30, 2016.

202. L. Luu, R. Saha, I. Parameshwaran, P. Saxena, and A. Hobor. On Power Splitting Games in Distributed Computation: the Case of Bitcoin Pooled Mining. In *2015 IEEE 28th Computer Security Foundations Symposium*, pages 397–411. IEEE, 2015.

203. L. Luu, J. Teutsch, R. Kulkarni, and P. Saxena. Demystifying Incentives in the Consensus Computer. In *Proceedings of the 22nd ACM SIGSAC Conference on Computer and Communications Security*, pages 706–719, 2015.

204. D. Malkhi, K. Nayak, and L. Ren. Flexible Byzantine Fault Tolerance. In *Proceedings of the 2019 ACM SIGSAC Conference on Computer and Communications Security*, pages 1041–1053, 2019.

205. J.-P. Martin and L. Alvisi. Fast Byzantine Paxos. In *Proceedings of the International Conference on Dependable Systems and Networks*, pages 402–411, 2004.

206. W. Martino, M. Quaintance, and S. Popejoy. Chainweb: a Proof-Of-Work Parallel-Chain Architecture for Massive Throughput. *Chainweb Whitepaper*, 19, 2018.

207. T. McConaghy, R. Marques, A. Müller, D. De Jonghe, T. McConaghy, G. McMullen, R. Henderson, S. Bellemare, and A. Granzotto. Bigchaindb: a Scalable Blockchain Database. *white paper, BigChainDB*, 2016.

208. T. McGhin, K.-K. R. Choo, C. Z. Liu, and D. He. Blockchain in Healthcare Applications: Research Challenges and Opportunities. *Journal of Network and Computer Applications*, 135:62–75, 2019.

209. R. C. Merkle. A Digital Signature Based on a Conventional Encryption Function. In C. Pomerance, editor, *Advances in Cryptology (CRYPTO '87)*, pages 369–378, Berlin, Heidelberg, 1988. Springer Berlin Heidelberg.

210. M. Mettler. Blockchain Technology in Healthcare: the Revolution Starts Here. In *2016 IEEE 18th international conference on e-health networking, applications and services (Healthcom)*, pages 1–3. IEEE, 2016.

211. A. Miller, A. Juels, E. Shi, B. Parno, and J. Katz. Permacoin: Repurposing Bitcoin Work for Data Preservation. In *2014 IEEE Symposium on Security and Privacy*, pages 475–490. IEEE, 2014.

212. A. Miller and J. J. LaViola Jr. Anonymous Byzantine Consensus From Moderately-Hard Puzzles: a Model for Bitcoin. *Available on line:* http://nakamotoinstitute.org/research/anonymous-byzantine-consensus, 2014.

213. A. Miller, Y. Xia, K. Croman, E. Shi, and D. Song. The Honey Badger of Bft Protocols. In *Proceedings of the 2016 ACM SIGSAC Conference on Computer and Communications Security*, pages 31–42, 2016.

214. C. Mohan. Tutorial: Blockchains and Databases. *Proceedings of the VLDB Endowment*, 10(12):2000–2001, 2017.

215. C. Mohan. Blockchains and Databases: a New Era in Distributed Computing. In *2018 IEEE 34th international conference on data engineering (ICDE)*, pages 1739–1740. IEEE, 2018.

216. C. Mohan, B. C. Ooi, and G. Vossen. Distributed Computing With Permissioned Blockchains and Databases (Dagstuhl Seminar 19261). In *Dagstuhl Reports*, volume 9. Schloss Dagstuhl-Leibniz-Zentrum fuer Informatik, 2019.

217. D. Mohanty. *R3 Corda for Architects and Developers: With Case Studies in Finance, Insurance, Healthcare, Travel, Telecom, and Agriculture*. Apress, 2019.

218. H. Moniz. The Istanbul Bft Consensus Algorithm. *arXiv preprint* arXiv:2002.03613, 2020.

219. A. Mostefaoui, H. Moumen, and M. Raynal. Signature-free Asynchronous Byzantine Consensus With T < N/3 and O (N2) Messages. In *Proceedings of the 2014 ACM symposium on Principles of distributed computing*, pages 2–9, 2014.

220. S. Nakamoto. Bitcoin: a Peer-To-Peer Electronic Cash System. *Decentralized Business Review*, page 21260, 2008.

221. Q. Nasir, I. A. Qasse, M. Abu Talib, and A. B. Nassif. Performance Analysis of Hyperledger Fabric Platforms. *Security and Communication Networks*, 2018, 2018.

222. S. Nathan, C. Govindarajan, A. Saraf, M. Sethi, and P. Jayachandran. Blockchain Meets Database: Design and Implementation of a Blockchain Relational Database. *PVLDB*, 12(11):1539–1552, 2019.

223. K. Nayak, S. Kumar, A. Miller, and E. Shi. Stubborn Mining: Generalizing Selfish Mining and Combining With An Eclipse Attack. In *2016 IEEE European Symposium on Security and Privacy (EuroS&P)*, pages 305–320. IEEE, 2016.

224. T. D. Neha Narula. "lecture 13: Payment Channels & the Lightning Network". In *Cryptocurrency Engineering and Design*. Cambridge MA, 2018. MIT OpenCourseWare.

225. G.-T. Nguyen and K. Kim. A Survey About Consensus Algorithms Used in Blockchain. *Journal of Information processing systems*, 14(1):101–128, 2018.

226. I. Nikolić, A. Kolluri, I. Sergey, P. Saxena, and A. Hobor. Finding the Greedy Prodigal and Suicidal Contracts At Scale. In *Proceedings of the 34th Annual Computer Security Applications Conference*, pages 653–663, 2018.

227. D. Ongaro and J. Ousterhout. In Search of An Understandable Consensus Algorithm. In *Proc. of USENIX Annual Technical Conference*, pages 305–320, 2014.

228. M. T. Özsu and P. Valduriez. *Principles of Distributed Database Systems*. Springer Science, 2020.

229. R. Pass, L. Seeman, and A. Shelat. Analysis of the Blockchain Protocol in Asynchronous Networks. In *Annual International Conference on the Theory and Applications of Cryptographic Techniques*, pages 643–673. Springer, 2017.

230. R. Pass and E. Shi. Thunderella: Blockchains With Optimistic Instant Confirmation. In *Annual International Conference on the Theory and Applications of Cryptographic Techniques*, pages 3–33. Springer, 2018.

231. D. Pavithran and R. Thomas. A Survey on Analyzing Bitcoin Transactions. In *2018 Fifth HCT Information Technology Trends (ITT)*, pages 227–231. IEEE, 2018.

232. A. Pavlovics. Jpmorgan's Quorum Blockchain Performance Testing, 2021.

233. Y. Peng, M. Du, F. Li, R. Cheng, and D. Song. Falcondb: Blockchain-Based Collaborative Database. In *Proc. of ACM SIGMOD International Conference on Management of Data*, pages 637–652, 2020.

234. S. Pongnumkul, C. Siripanpornchana, and S. Thajchayapong. Performance Analysis of Private Blockchain Platforms in Varying Workloads. In *2017 26th International Conference on Computer Communication and Networks (ICCCN)*, pages 1–6. IEEE, 2017.

235. J. Poon and V. Buterin. Plasma: Scalable Autonomous Smart Contracts. *White paper*, pages 1–47, 2017.

236. J. Poon and T. Dryja. The Bitcoin Lightning Network: Scalable Off-Chain Instant Payments, 2016.

237. K. Qin, L. Zhou, and A. Gervais. Quantifying Blockchain Extractable Value: How Dark Is the Forest? *arXiv preprint* arXiv:2101.05511, 2021.

238. H. Qureshi. A Hacker Stole 31M of Ether-How It Happened and What It Means for Ethereum. *Freecodecamp. org, Jul*, 20:2017, 2017.

239. F. Reid and M. Harrigan. An Analysis of Anonymity in the Bitcoin System. In *Security and privacy in social networks*, pages 197–223. Springer, 2013.

240. D. Reijsbergen and T. T. A. Dinh. On Exploiting Transaction Concurrency To Speed Up Blockchains. In *2020 IEEE 40th International Conference on Distributed Computing Systems (ICDCS)*, pages 1044–1054. IEEE, 2020.

241. L. Ren. Analysis of Nakamoto Consensus. *IACR Cryptol. ePrint Arch.*, 2019:943, 2019.

242. F. Ritz and A. Zugenmaier. The Impact of Uncle Rewards on Selfish Mining in Ethereum. In *2018 IEEE European Symposium on Security and Privacy Workshops (EuroS&PW)*, pages 50–57. IEEE, 2018.

243. T. Rocket, M. Yin, K. Sekniqi, R. van Renesse, and E. G. Sirer. Scalable and Probabilistic Leaderless Bft Consensus Through Metastability. *arXiv preprint* arXiv:1906.08936, 2019.

244. D. Ron and A. Shamir. Quantitative Analysis of the Full Bitcoin Transaction Graph. In *International Conference on Financial Cryptography and Data Security*, pages 6–24. Springer, 2013.

245. S. Rouhani and R. Deters. Performance Analysis of Ethereum Transactions in Private Blockchain. In *2017 8th IEEE International Conference on Software Engineering and Service Science (ICSESS)*, pages 70–74. IEEE, 2017.

246. P. Ruan, G. Chen, T. T. A. Dinh, Q. Lin, B. C. Ooi, and M. Zhang. Fine-grained Secure and Efficient Data Provenance on Blockchain Systems. *Proceedings of the VLDB Endowment*, 12(9):975–988, 2019.

247. P. Ruan, T. T. A. Dinh, D. Loghin, M. Zhang, G. Chen, Q. Lin, and B. C. Ooi. Blockchains vs. Distributed Databases: Dichotomy and Fusion. In *Proceedings of the 2021 International Conference on Management of Data*, pages 1504–1517, 2021.

248. P. Ruan, D. Loghin, Q.-T. Ta, M. Zhang, G. Chen, and B. C. Ooi. A Transactional Perspective on Execute-Order-Validate Blockchains. In *Proc. of ACM SIGMOD International Conference on Management of Data*, pages 543–557, 2020.

249. M. Saad, L. Njilla, C. Kamhoua, and A. Mohaisen. Countering Selfish Mining in Blockchains. In *2019 International Conference on Computing, Networking and Communications (ICNC)*, pages 360–364. IEEE, 2019.

250. S. Saberi, M. Kouhizadeh, J. Sarkis, and L. Shen. Blockchain Technology and Its Relationships To Sustainable Supply Chain Management. *International Journal of Production Research*, 57(7):2117–2135, 2019.

251. F. Saleh. Blockchain Without Waste: Proof-Of-Stake. *The Review of financial studies*, 34(3):1156–1190, 2021.

252. F. Santos and V. Kostakis. The Dao: a Million Dollar Lesson in Blockchain Governance. *School of Business and Governance, Ragnar Nurkse Department of Innovation and Governance*, 2018.

253. A. Sapirshtein, Y. Sompolinsky, and A. Zohar. Optimal Selfish Mining Strategies in Bitcoin. In *International Conference on Financial Cryptography and Data Security*, pages 515–532. Springer, 2016.

254. V. Saraph and M. Herlihy. An Empirical Study of Speculative Concurrency in Ethereum Smart Contracts. *arXiv preprint* arXiv:1901.01376, 2019.

255. M. Schäffer, M. Di Angelo, and G. Salzer. Performance and Scalability of Private Ethereum Blockchains. In *International Conference on Business Process Management*, pages 103–118. Springer, 2019.

256. F. M. Schuhknecht, A. Sharma, J. Dittrich, and D. Agrawal. Chainifydb: How To Get Rid of Your Blockchain and Use Your Dbms Instead. 2021.

257. I. Sergey and A. Hobor. A Concurrent Perspective on Smart Contracts. In *International Conference on Financial Cryptography and Data Security*, pages 478–493. Springer, 2017.

258. I. Sergey, V. Nagaraj, J. Johannsen, A. Kumar, A. Trunov, and K. C. G. Hao. Safer Smart Contract Programming With Scilla. *Proceedings of the ACM on Programming Languages*, 3(OOPSLA):1–30, 2019.

259. C. Sguanci, R. Spatafora, and A. M. Vergani. Layer 2 Blockchain Scaling: a Survey. *arXiv preprint* arXiv:2107.10881, 2021.

260. A. Sharma, F. M. Schuhknecht, D. Agrawal, and J. Dittrich. Blurring the Lines Between Blockchains and Database Systems: the Case of Hyperledger Fabric. In *Proc. of International Conference on Management of Data*, pages 105–122, 2019.

261. B. Shickel, P. J. Tighe, A. Bihorac, and P. Rashidi. Deep EHR: a Survey of Recent Advances in Deep Learning Techniques for Electronic Health Record (EHR) Analysis. *IEEE journal of biomedical and health informatics*, 22(5):1589–1604, 2017.

262. A. Shoker. Sustainable Blockchain Through Proof of Exercise. In *2017 IEEE 16th International Symposium on Network Computing and Applications (NCA)*, pages 1–9. IEEE, 2017.

263. Y. Sompolinsky and A. Zohar. Secure High-Rate Transaction Processing in Bitcoin. In *International Conference on Financial Cryptography and Data Security*, pages 507–527. Springer, 2015.

264. M. Stonebraker and L. A. Rowe. The Design of Postgres. *SIGMOD Rec.*, 15(2):340–355, 1986.

265. A. Tai, M. Wei, M. J. Freedman, I. Abraham, and D. Malkhi. Replex: a Scalable Highly Available Multi-Index Data Store. In *Usenix ATC*, 2016.

266. P. Thakkar and S. Natarajan. Scaling Hyperledger Fabric Using Pipelined Execution and Sparse Peers. *arXiv preprint* arXiv:2003.05113, 2020.

267. P. Thakkar, S. Nathan, and B. Viswanathan. Performance Benchmarking and Optimizing Hyperledger Fabric Blockchain Platform. In *Proc. of 26th International Symposium on Modeling, Analysis, and Simulation of Computer and Telecommunication Systems (MASCOTS)*, pages 264–276. IEEE, 2018.

268. S. Thomas and E. Schwartz. A Protocol for Interledger Payments. https://interledger.org/interledger.pdf, 2015.

269. J. Tinguely. Benchmarking of Distributed Ledger Technology. 2019.

270. D. K. Tosh, S. Shetty, X. Liang, C. A. Kamhoua, K. A. Kwiat, and L. Njilla. Security Implications of Blockchain Cloud With Analysis of Block Withholding Attack. In *2017 17th IEEE/ACM International Symposium on Cluster, Cloud and Grid Computing (CCGRID)*, pages 458–467. IEEE, 2017.

271. H. T. Vo, S. Wang, D. Agrawal, G. Chen, and B. C. Ooi. Logbase: a Scalable Log-Structured Database System in the Cloud. *Proc. of VLDB Endow.*, 5(10):1004–1015, June 2012.

272. Q. H. Vu, M. Lupu, and B. C. Ooi. *Peer-to-peer Computing: Principles and Applications.* Springer, 2010.

273. A. Vukotic, N. Watt, T. Abedrabbo, D. Fox, and J. Partner. *Neo4j in Action.* Manning Publications Co., 2014.

274. G. Wang, Z. J. Shi, M. Nixon, and S. Han. Sok: Sharding on Blockchain. In *Proceedings of the 1st ACM Conference on Advances in Financial Technologies*, pages 41–61, 2019.

275. J. Wang, X. Chen, X. Huang, I. You, and Y. Xiang. Verifiable Auditing for Outsourced Database in Cloud Computing. *IEEE transactions on computers*, 64(11):3293–3303, 2015.

276. J. Wang and H. Wang. Monoxide: Scale Out Blockchains With Asynchronous Consensus Zones. In *16th USENIX Symposium on Networked Systems Design and Implementation (NSDI 19)*, pages 95–112, 2019.

277. Q. Wang, J. Yu, S. Chen, and Y. Xiang. Sok: Diving Into Dag-Based Blockchain Systems. *arXiv preprint* arXiv:2012.06128, 2020.

278. S. Wang, T. T. A. Dinh, Q. Lin, Z. Xie, M. Zhang, Q. Cai, G. Chen, B. C. Ooi, and P. Ruan. Forkbase: An Efficient Storage Engine for Blockchain and Forkable Applications. *Proc. VLDB Endow.*, 11(10):1137-1150, June 2018.

279. W. Wang, D. T. Hoang, P. Hu, Z. Xiong, D. Niyato, P. Wang, Y. Wen, and D. I. Kim. A Survey on Consensus Mechanisms and Mining Strategy Management in Blockchain Networks. *IEEE Access*, 7:22328–22370, 2019.

280. M. Weber, G. Domeniconi, J. Chen, D. K. I. Weidele, C. Bellei, T. Robinson, and C. E. Leiserson. Anti-money Laundering in Bitcoin: Experimenting With Graph Convolutional Networks for Financial Forensics. *arXiv preprint* arXiv:1908.02591, 2019.

281. S. M. Werner, D. Perez, L. Gudgeon, A. Klages-Mundt, D. Harz, and W. J. Knottenbelt. Sok: Decentralized Finance (Defi). *arXiv preprint* arXiv:2101.08778, 2021.

282. G. Wood et al. Ethereum: a Secure Decentralised Generalised Transaction Ledger. *Ethereum project yellow paper*, 151(2014):1–32, 2014.

283. K. Wüst and A. Gervais. Do You Need a Blockchain? In *2018 Crypto Valley Conference on Blockchain Technology (CVCBT)*, pages 45–54. IEEE, 2018.

284. Y. Xiao, N. Zhang, W. Lou, and Y. T. Hou. A Survey of Distributed Consensus Protocols for Blockchain Networks. *IEEE Communications Surveys & Tutorials*, 22(2):1432–1465, 2020.

285. Z. Xie, Q. Cai, H. Jagadish, B. C. Ooi, and W. F. Wong. Parallelizing Skip Lists for In-Memory Multi-Core Database Systems. In *2017 IEEE 33rd International Conference on Data Engineering (ICDE)*, pages 119–122. IEEE, 2017.

286. D. Yaga, P. Mell, N. Roby, and K. Scarfone. Blockchain Technology Overview. Technical report, National Institute of Standards and Technology, 2018.

287. A. Yakovenko. Solana: A new architecture for a high performance blockchain v0. 8.13. *Whitepaper*, 2018.

288. X. Yang, Y. Zhang, S. Wang, B. Yu, F. Li, Y. Li, and W. Yan. Ledgerdb: a Centralized Ledger Database for Universal Audit and Verification. *Proc. of VLDB Endow.*, 13(12):3138–3151, 2020.

289. M. Yin, D. Malkhi, M. K. Reiter, G. G. Gueta, and I. Abraham. Hotstuff: Bft Consensus With Linearity and Responsiveness. In *Proc. of ACM Symposium on Principles of Distributed Computing*, pages 347–356, 2019.

290. H. Yu, I. Nikolić, R. Hou, and P. Saxena. Ohie: Blockchain Scaling Made Simple. In *2020 IEEE Symposium on Security and Privacy (SP)*, pages 90–105. IEEE, 2020.

291. C. Yue, T. T. A. Dinh, Z. Xie, M. Zhang, G. Chen, B. C. Ooi, and X. Xiao. LedgeBase: A Distributed Verifiable Ledger Database. Technical report, National University of Singapore, 2022.

292. V. Zakhary, D. Agrawal, and A. E. Abbadi. Atomic Commitment Across Blockchains. *arXiv preprint* arXiv:1905.02847, 2019.

293. M. Zamani, M. Movahedi, and M. Raykova. Rapidchain: Scaling Blockchain Via Full Sharding. In *Proceedings of the 2018 ACM SIGSAC Conference on Computer and Communications Security*, pages 931–948, 2018.

294. A. Zamyatin, M. Al-Bassam, D. Zindros, E. Kokoris-Kogias, P. Moreno-Sanchez, A. Kiayias, and W. J. Knottenbelt. Sok: Communication Across Distributed Ledgers. 2019.

295. D. A. Zetzsche, D. W. Arner, and R. P. Buckley. Decentralized Finance. *Journal of Financial Regulation*, 6(2):172–203, 2020.

296. M. Zhang, Z. Xie, C. Yue, and Z. Zhong. Spitz: a Verifiable Database System. *Proc. of VLDB Endow.*, 13(12):3449–3460, Aug. 2020.

297. P. Zhang, D. C. Schmidt, J. White, and G. Lenz. Blockchain Technology Use Cases in Healthcare. In *Advances in computers*, volume 111, pages 1–41. Elsevier, 2018.

298. Y. Zhang, J. Katz, and C. Papamanthou. Integridb: Verifiable Sql for Outsourced Databases. In *Proc. of 22nd ACM SIGSAC Conference on Computer and Communications Security*, pages 1480–1491, 2015.

299. Z. Zheng, S. Xie, H.-N. Dai, X. Chen, and H. Wang. Blockchain Challenges and Opportunities: a Survey. *International Journal of Web and Grid Services*, 14(4):352–375, 2018.

300. Q. Zhou, H. Huang, Z. Zheng, and J. Bian. Solutions To Scalability of Blockchain: a Survey. *IEEE Access*, 8:16440–16455, 2020.

301. R. B. Zur, I. Eyal, and A. Tamar. Efficient Mdp Analysis for Selfish-Mining in Blockchains. In *Proceedings of the 2nd ACM Conference on Advances in Financial Technologies*, pages 113–131, 2020.

Printed in the United States
by Baker & Taylor Publisher Services